Exploring the Depths of Cognitive Psychology:

Understanding the Mind's Inner Workings.

By

James schend

Table of Contents

Chapter 1

Introduction

1.1 Overview of Cognitive Evolution

a general framework of cognitive evolution. To start, cognitive evolution refers to the evolutionary modifications in the mind and discernment that have transpired throughout mankind's collection of experiences. It's a large topic, although I may try to cover the key focuses and successes of cognitive evolution.

Alright, to get underway then, I'll start with the nuts and bolts of human evolution. The first known human progenitors, the Australopithecus, evolved in Africa roughly a long time ago. Their thoughts were a lot more modest than present-day individuals', nevertheless, they possessed a few cognitive skills, like employing gadgets and taking care of troubles. Then, at that point, about a long time ago, the Homo habilis evolved, and they had significantly more noteworthy cognitive skills, including language and iconic notions. These early individuals began to pursue and seek food, and their cognitive skills helped them to adapt to new surroundings and beat problems. Does it sound like a good beginning?

Human Great! As cognitive development evolved, the Homo erectus appeared roughly 1.8 a long time ago, and their brains were around the same size as contemporary day humans. They possessed substantially more noteworthy cognitive powers, individuals'; increased critical thinking abilities, social understanding, and conceptual reasoning. The Homo erectus were fast to migrate out of Africa, and they expanded to many places on the earth, including Asia and Europe.

Alright, so then, at that point, we got the Homo neanderthalensis, which emerged approximately a long time ago in Europe and Asia. They had far great contemporary-day the Homo erectus, and they were adept toolmakers, trackers, and foragers. They also possessed sophisticated social designs and established rituals, craftsmanship, and language. They coincided with the Homo sapiens, who evolved close to a long time ago in Africa. The

Homo sapiens, or current-day humans, exhibited substantially greater intelligence than the Homo neanderthalensis, and they had far more sophisticated cognitive skills, including complex language, innovativeness, and awareness. They are OK, we should leap ahead to the Cognitive Revolution, which began something like quite a time ago. This was a crucial defining event in cognitive development, and it was marked apart by a vital expansion in imagination, distinctive thinking, and representational style of acting. During this age, humans began to produce handicrafts, music, and complex equipment. people also evolved more complicated language, and people began to construct imaginations, tales, and religions. Does it sound like a key phase in cognitive evolution?

Amazing! Then, we have the Agrarian Revolution, which began close to a long time ago. This was one more key defining point, and it was set apart by the move from agricultural social orders to established farming social organizations. With farming came the expansion of additional mind-boggling social arrangements, with the division of labor, social progressive systems, and metropolitan regions. These progressions also enormously altered cognitive development, prompting increased advancement, specialization, and partnership. Magnificent! With the Cognitive Revolution and the Agrarian Revolution, individuals achieved huge headways in their cognitive capabilities. However, cognitive growth didn't end there - the Modern Revolution, which began in the eighteenth 100 years, also substantially changed human discernment. The invention of machines, new sources of energy, and big-scale production all inspired much more remarkable breakthroughs in cognitive capabilities. People turned out to be more particular and more industrious, and they had the choice to encourage far more complicated inventions.

The framework of cognitive evolution studies the remarkable excursion of human understanding throughout evolutionary timeframes. This portion delves into the growth and development of cognitive skills, containing major successes and various techniques that have fashioned the human brain. From early cognitive skills in genealogy individuals to the nuances of contemporary day cognitive challenges, this sketch provides space for a thorough exploration of cognitive development, establishing linkages between natural, social, and mechanical consequences.

1.2 Importance of investigating cognitive evolution

Studying cognitive development is vital as it gives insight into the origins and varied parts of human knowledge. By disentangling the processes that produced cognitive capabilities over generations, we acquire insight into the main aspects of the human way of acting, critical thinking, and social communications. Understanding cognitive evolution also has pragmatic implications, enlightening domains like training, brain research, and innovation, directing us in tending to current challenges and equipping the possibility for extra cognitive improvement later on.

1. **Understanding Human Uniqueness:** Studying cognitive evolution unwinds what makes human cognizance unique and how it has expanded strikingly across animals.

2. **Insights into Hereditary Behavior:** Cognitive evolution gives insight into the cognitive skills required for durability and proliferation in our

forebears, offering experiences into their methods of acting.

3. **Adaptation to Changing Environments:** Inspecting cognitive evolution provides us with an understanding of how human cognizance changed to varied settings, from ancestral scenes to modern-day, innovation-driven societal regimes.

4. **Medical and Mental Implications:** Bits of information regarding cognitive evolution contribute to comprehending cognitive difficulties, suggesting plausible applications in medicines and brain science.

5. **Advancements in Education:** Understanding how comprehension advances support building attractive instructive methods that line up with the regular movement of cognitive capabilities in individuals.

6. **Technological Innovation:** Cognitive evolution study advises the strategy regarding simple-to-use improvements, taking into consideration how individuals process info and collaborate with their existing condition.

7. **Evolutionary Premise of Social Behavior:** Looking into cognitive evolution offers an introduction to comprehending the basic

foundations of puzzling social ways of behavior and relationships among individuals.

8. **Predicting Future Cognitive Trends:** By researching cognitive evolution, we obtain pieces of information regarding prospective future cognitive patterns, anticipating problems and astounding open doors in human cognitive turn of events.

9. **Cultural Evolution and Knowledge Transfer:** Cognitive evolution research helps to understand how knowledge and social behaviors are transported across eras, affecting cultural evolution.

10. **Ethical and Moral Considerations:** Experiences from cognitive evolution enhance talks

on morality and ethical character, offering a basis for understanding the evolutionary beginning points of human qualities and dynamic cycles.

Chapter 2

The Evolutionary Framework

2.1 Darwinian Perspectives on Cognitive Development

A transformational system relates to a calculated construction or imaginary perspective that is developed in the criteria of development. It offers a focal point through which diverse idiosyncrasies, cycles, or frameworks may be recognized, evaluated, and made sense of within the formulation of developmental norms. This structure incorporates a scope of disciplines, from science and hereditary qualities to brain research, culture, and then some, offering a bound together way to deal with figuring out the variety, improvement, and interconnectedness of living creatures and their characteristics over the long haul.

At its heart, a transformational structure is strongly impacted by the key concepts brought forth by Charles Darwin in his theory of development by normal determination. This theory posits that species evolve over ages by the differential endurance and proliferation of individuals with advantageous features, prompting the gradual modification of populaces to their surroundings.

From a broader viewpoint, a transformational system reaches out beyond science to embrace diverse sectors where transformative principles are used to make sense of instances, changes, and advances. For instance, revolutionary brain science studies how human behavior and mental cycles have progressed over the long haul, whereas social development investigates the transmission and transformation of social practices across millennia.

Key aspects of a developmental framework include:

1. **Historical Context:** Recognizing the real progress of species and features over geographical time, detecting the effect of historical circumstances and decision conflicts.

2. **Adaptation:** Accentuating the concept that living organisms have qualities that have formed as

changes to their environmental specialty, bringing advantages to persistence and generation.

3. **Variation and Selection:** Perceiving the importance of hereditary variation within populaces and how normal determination follows up on this variety, prompting alterations in the recurrence of qualities throughout the ages.

4. **Transmission of Traits:** Understanding how hereditary data is conveyed beginning with one age and then onto the next and how social data is delivered in human social orders.

5. **Interconnectedness:** Valuing the interrelated notion of life, where modifications in a single area

of a biological system or animal groupings might have progressively increasing impacts, altering the more extensive developing scene.

6. **Dynamic Nature:** Perceiving that development is a progressive, dynamic interaction and that the particular powers following up on populaces might alter after some time due to ecological movements or other circumstances.

Fundamentally, a transformational framework delivers a fundamental grasp of the cycles that have sculpted the diversity of life, presenting a linked together worldview that rises beyond separate specialties. It enables a thorough examination of how life has grown and remains growing across numerous sizes, from the sub-atomic level to surroundings and societal frameworks.

Charles Darwin's Transformative Points of View: Revealing the Components of Life's Diversity

Charles Darwin, a name inseparable from the progressive idea of evolution, continually modified's perception humans may interpret life's diversity. His hefty essay, "On the Beginning of Species," issued in 1859, created a revolution in viewpoint in science by providing a method through which animal categories arise after some time. Darwin's ideas, reflected in the theory of progress by regular determination, have had important repercussions in science as well as in creating our sense of the interconnectivity and dynamic nature of life on The planet.

Verifiable Setting

To appreciate the importance of Darwin's developmental perspectives, it's important to delve into the genuine environment of the mid-nineteenth 100 years. The overarching concept was one of fixity of animal types, where animals were considered as permanent representations. Darwin's journey on board HMS Beagle, notably his impressions of diverse animals in the Galápagos Islands, sparked a breakthrough viewpoint. He studied the conventional tale and began off on a logical study that would question established forth criteria.

Center Standards of Darwinian Advancement

1. **Natural Choice: The Driving Force**

At the basis of Darwin's developmental points of view is the notion of regular determination. This component functions as a non-irregular interaction whereby persons with noteworthy attributes for durability and propagation are obligated to give those characteristics to the future. Over the long run, this unequal accomplishment prompts the progressive modification of populaces to their surroundings. Regular decision fills in as the major impetus behind the diversity and complexity observed in living biological beings.

2. **Variation, Legacy, and Differential Reproduction**

Darwin realized the relevance of heterogeneity within populaces. People display differences in traits, and a part of these variants are heritable, going from parent to progeny. In the contest for presence, not all persons have similar powers of endurance and multiplication. Those with traits better suitable to their existing scenario are bound to leave posterity, thus maintaining explicit attributes in subsequent centuries.

3. **Historical Setting: Charles Darwin and "On the Beginning of Species"**

Darwin's opus, "On the Beginning of Species," offered an elaborate synthesis of his concepts. Distributed after quite a while of meticulous investigation and analysis, the book spread out the evidence for improvement and described the norms of regular choosing. It framed the provable progress of species, highlighting the job of transformation to shifting situations in creating the diversity of existence.

Applications to Science

1. **Evolutionary Science: Binding Together Principle**
Darwinian evolution fills in as a tying-together standard in research, supplying a framework to figure out the links between diverse species. It forms

the basis of modern transformational research, driving inquiry in disciplines, for example, phylogenetics, near-life structures, and sub-atomic science. Developmental standards are used to detangle the common family and difference of species, delivering encounters into the diverse snare of existence.

2. **Examples of Darwinian Development in Action**

Perceptions and research across diverse organic frameworks furnish ample substantiation of Darwinian progression. From the typical illustration of the peppered moths throughout the Modern Upset to the documented instances of anti-toxin blockage in microorganisms, illustrations of regular choice-generating populaces are many. These models demonstrate the adaptable notion of development in light of developing situations.

3. **Criticisms and Contentions: Expanding the Paradigm**

While Darwin's experiences were progressive, the subject of developmental science has not remained stagnant. Progressing research has enlarged and enhanced the first viewpoint. Challenges, including the reconciliation of hereditary attributes into developmental hypothesis, the job of amplified balance in speciation, and the inquiry of widened transformational combination, mirror the unique notion of logical request. Darwinian development provides an established, although modern opinions combine fresh knowledge and resolve obstructions.

Human Development

1. **Hominid Development: Following Ancestry**

One of the most bewitching utilizations of Darwinian progress is in the area of human development. Fossil disclosures, relative living systems, and hereditary evidence have helped researchers to track the developmental excursion from our usual ancestors with distinct monkeys to the advent of Homo sapiens. The norms of natural selection are visible in the variances that formed primate species north of millions of years.

2. **Key Fossils and Discoveries**

The unearthing of fossils like "Lucy" (Australopithecus afarensis) and the continual disclosures in areas like the Fracture Valley have supplied crucial insights into our developing history. These fossils, with their physical components and date, contribute to the mosaic of data demonstrating the steady progression of human features over successive periods.

3. **Behavioral Development: From Australopithecines to Current Humans**

Past real modifications and Darwinian ideas reach out to the growth of the human method of functioning. The advancement of cognitive skills, social designs, and complicated social practices should be evident as diverse answers to the challenges confronted by genealogical populaces. The interrelated evolution of physical and social features demonstrates the journey from Australopithecus to the present Homo sapien.

All in all, Charles Darwin's developmental points of view, represented in the notion of progress by natural selection, have gone beyond the bounds of science to impact our knowledge of life itself. The norms of natural selection, diversity, and transformation shape the core of modern developmental research, offering a coming-together system that transcends numerous fields. From the verified context that stimulated Darwin's inquiries to the vast applicability in disciplines like human development, his inheritance resounds in the continual research of life's intricate embroidered artwork. Darwin's views have weathered daily hardship as well as carry on progressing as current inquiry deepens and refines our comprehension of the instruments that underpin life's diversity.

2.2 Natural Selection and Cognitive Traits: The Versatile Woven Artwork of Human Intelligence**

Natural selection, a basis of Darwinian growth, stretches its effect beyond real qualities to mold the many-sided terrain of cognitive traits in humans. The interchange between ecological challenges and the demand for flexible responses has impacted the evolution of the human mind. Looking at cognitive qualities from the standpoint of natural selection offers a tale of endurance advantage, critical thinking capacity, and the innovative understanding that has helped Homo sapiens to explore complex social arrangements and dynamic environments.

Transformation of Cognitive Traits:

Natural selection operates on the heritable variation existing within a population, leaning toward features that strengthen an organic entity's ability to make due and recur. On account of cognitive qualities, this flexible cycle is noticeable in the expansion of crucial capacities to consider, memory keeping, and social understanding. These cognitive boundaries have been honed over revolutionary time, delivering clear advantages to humans in their partnerships with the environment and various individuals from their species.

Endurance Advantage:

The cognitive qualities leaned toward natural selection are those that give an endurance advantage. For early humans, the skill to promptly inspect and respond to hazards in the climate was crucial. Improved cognitive capacities, for example, heightened situational attention, fast direction, and the ability to gain from encounters, supplied a fair advantage in investigating the problems of the genetic environment. People with these cognitive qualities were obligated to remain away from hazards and safeguard possessions, adding to their increased possibilities of endurance and multiplication.

Social Intelligence:**

The progress of human social designs further underscores the function of natural selection in shaping cognitive qualities. Social cooperations create complicated issues that demand a contemporary comprehension of others' aims, sentiments, and motivations. People with enhanced social insight, typified by compassion, cooperation, and effective communication, were better positioned to create relationships, lay down friendly ties, and investigate the unexpected parts of shared life. Such cognitive skills boosted the possibility of efficient cooperation within meetings, contributing to the regenerative improvement of people holding these adaptable features.

Device Use and Cognitive Complexity:

The utilization of instruments addresses a major element of human cognitive growth generated by natural selection. The ability to develop and communicate instruments necessitates improved cognitive capacities, for example, critical thinking, organizing, and spatial reasoning. Early individuals who succeeded in these cognitive boundaries received advantages in acquiring food, constructing cover, and changing to varied situations. Subsequently, the cognitive features connected with equipment usage got embedded in the transformational embroidery, contributing to the distinctive cognitive capacities of Homo sapiens.

Social Transmission of Cognitive Skills:

Natural selection acts on inherited diversity as well as extends out to social activities. The transfer of knowledge, talents, and cognitive processes via social channels is based upon certain conflicts. Cognitive qualities that operate with effective learning, mimicry, and variation to changing social settings are leaned upon. The ability to acquire and communicate information socially affords a fresh avenue to the evolution of cognitive qualities, letting the human species amass aggregate knowledge over eons.

Current Implications:

In the present situation, the tradition of natural selection on cognitive qualities remains visible. While the challenges confronted by humans have progressed, the cognitive constraints refined over millennia remain influencing individual and cultural replies. From studying the nuances of modern innovation to addressing social and ecological concerns, the adaptability and critical thinking talents instilled in human awareness reflect the persisting influence of natural selection.

Natural selection, as a key drive in growth, has complicatedly woven cognitive qualities into the texture of human knowledge. The flexible notion of cognitive growth, established by the problems of endurance, social factors, and societal complexity, has endowed Homo sapiens with an amazing cognitive capacity. Understanding cognitive features from the viewpoint of natural selection offers experiences into the transformational past as well as a foundation for appreciating the complexity of the human brain in the present day.

Chapter 3

Early Cognitive Milestones

3.1 Primitive Cognitive Functions in Ancestral Humans: Tracing the Roots of Human Intelligence**

The mental excursion of Homo sapiens is thoroughly embedded in the developing woven artwork, where rudimentary mental powers built the framework for the astounding knowledge that defines present individuals. As we study the early mental accomplishments of our tribal ancestors, we delve into the mental changes that were crucial for endurance in the tough circumstances of ancient times.

1. **Perception and Tangible Awareness:**

At the core of basic mental capacities among tribal people was a profound dependency on discernment and palpable attentiveness. Early individuals needed to explore complicated and often perilous situations, where the skill to understand concrete hints was fundamental for survival. Elevated optical acuity, acute hearing, and a strong perception of smell were crucial for spotting prospective hazards like hunters or differentiating wellsprings of food and water.

These concrete skills were crucial for individual endurance as well as assumed a key position in group vibrations. The exchanging of non-verbal indications via glances, non-verbal communication, and vocalizations contributed to the union of gathers, functioning with cooperation and aggregate protection against exterior hazards.

2. **Memory for Survival:**

Without composed language and complicated outside stockpiling systems, household people are strongly reliant on remembering as an essential mental talent for durability. The remembering capacity the locations of water supplies, the sorts of plants that were tasty, and the methods of behaving of both prey and hunters was vital.

Early humans established sturdy verbal and spatial memory frameworks, letting them mentally arrange their contextual components, examine earlier encounters, and plan future actions. Memory, in this basic arrangement, is filled in as a mental compass, permitting individuals to decide on educated opinions regarding asset utilization, movement patterns, and expected threats.

3. **Basic Critical thinking Skills:**

The issues faced by family folks demanded crucial critical thinking talents as a primary mental success. From constructing simple tools for hunting and ensuring to concocting methods for helpful hunting or sanctuary construction, early humans demonstrated a limit about critical thinking that was unexpectedly related to their endurance.

These rudimentary critical thinking abilities needed a combination of observational learning, experimentation, and social interaction. The mental flexibility to alter replies for varied contexts was crucial in a strong atmosphere where obstacles were different and continually changing.

4. **Spatial Thinking and Navigation:**

The traveling style of life of genealogical people needed advanced spatial thinking and route talents. Following periodic changes, figuring out the geography of their environmental elements, and preparing relocation routes were key aspects of endurance. Early humans demonstrated a natural aptitude to mentally organize their existing condition, understand milestones, and work out spatial linkages, contributing to their development in exploring diverse settings.

Spatial thinking also assumed an essential position in endeavors like effective hunting or avoiding hunters. The mental planning of areas and the ability to cognitively project and manage geographical data were crucial aspects of early human discernment.

5. **Social Insight and Helpful Living:**

The acquisition of social consciousness marked great mental success in hereditary individuals. Living in gatherings gave many advantages, including acceptable hunting, protection from hunters, and shared childcare tasks. Early individuals demonstrated current knowledge of societal progressive systems, familial connection links, and general sentiments.

Crude social awareness featured the recognition of individual personalities within a gathering, the translation of important gestures, and the ability to truly coordinate. This fundamental social understanding created the basis for the sophisticated social designs and relationships witnessed in current human social organizations.

6. **Language Precursors:**

While language in its sophisticated structure emerged a lot later, genealogical individuals demonstrated early language forerunners that operated with correspondence. Vocalizations, signs, and a basic symbolic language for the exchanging of data within gatherings. Early people passed on vital needs, communicated info about the environment, and created group workouts via these rudimentary sorts of communication.

These early linguistic antecedents filled in as apparatuses for collaborative effort, allowing more proficient planning and execution of assignments. The enhancement of language, even in its early beginnings, addressed a mental feat that substantially altered the path of human progress.

7. **Emotional Guideline and Empathy:**

Crude mental capacities in tribal people included close-to-home guidelines and the limit of compassion. Close-to-home sensations, including fear, joy, or indignation, played a big position in fast endurance responses. Furthermore, the ability to grasp and address the sentiments of individuals within the gathering promoted engagement, fortitude, and shared care obligations.

Compassion, even in its basic forms, helped the evolution of gatherings by developing altruistic ways of behaving, shared aid, and the creation of strong social relationships. This rudimentary ability to appreciate others on a deeper level established the groundwork for the mind-boggling profound sceneries observed in human cooperations today.

The basic mental parts of ancestral people were carefully honed by the stresses of their environment, representing a remarkable metamorphosis to the challenges of endurance. These early mental successes outlined the cause for the expansion of human knowledge, providing for the improvement of subsequently evolved mental cycles across ages. While these capacities would seem to be uncomplicated by modern standards, they address the fundamental mental tool stockpile that enabled our progenitors to grow in various and required settings. Understanding these rudimentary mental talents offers a glance into the origins of human understanding and the many-sided mental excursion that has developed the cutting-edge human brain.

3.2 Tool Use and Cognitive Advancements: Unraveling the Evolution of Human Intelligence**

Device utilization stays as a characteristic highlight in the tale of human evolution, designating a critical second when cerebral progressions interlaced with physical mastery, molding the direction of Homo sapiens. The ability to construct, ace, and employ devices not only reflected a varied response to the challenges of the environment however in addition declared a mental turmoil that set the preparation for the growth of human knowing.

1. **The Beginning of Hardware Use: A Mental Leap**

The arrival of hardware usage addresses a large mental leap in the developmental excursion of primates. While diverse animals demonstrate gadget usage to variable degrees, the sophistication and adaptability of human tools put Homo sapiens distinct. The first instruments developed by our forefathers were extremely simple, composed of basic stones altered for stated purposes. The capability to observe, choose, and regulate items for an ideal outcome exhibited a degree of mental agility and a crucial ability to think that identified early individuals.

2. **Cognitive Adaptability and Issue Solving:**
Instrument utilization involves mental adaptability — the capability to change and use numerous

methods in light of the requirements of a specified task. Early individuals are required to scan their existing scenario, grasp the probable objectives of available supplies, and develop replies to overcome challenges. This mental flexibility prompted the manufacture of instruments as well as provided the basis for critical thinking skills that turned out to be increasingly mind-boggling as apparatuses improved.

The iterative phase of hardware improvement needed observational learning, trial and error, and the ability to adjust systems given findings. Mental headways in recognizing situations and logical effects, foreseeing outcomes, and refining approaches assumed a crucial role in the refinement of gadgets across ages.

3. **Spatial Cognizance and Planning:**
Creating and utilizing devices require many-sided spatial sensing and arrangement. Early individuals are expected to conceptually conceive the ideal ultimate result, arrange the grouping of tasks necessary, and execute these operations with precision. Spatial thinking assumed a fundamental role in molding equipment for specified capabilities, whether it was constructing a sharp edge for cutting or a point for hunting.

The improvement of tools also needed an understanding of the actual qualities of materials, for example, recognizing which pebbles were acceptable for knapping or which woods were finest for handles. This dominance of spatial connections and material attributes demonstrated developed mental skills that created the framework for more sophisticated critical thinking activities.

4. **Cultural Transmission of Hardware Knowledge:**

The significance of hardware utilization goes out beyond individual mental headways; it defines an extension of natural and social growth. Early individuals passed on genetic data as well as transmitted knowledge regarding equipment-producing procedures socially. This social transfer of hardware knowledge addresses a unique mental change, where gaining from others developed into an urgent component of endurance and variety.

As instrument-producing approaches were discussed inside gatherings, they became social practices, developing and altering over the long stretch. This path of social growth regarded the accumulation of collective knowledge, where headways in apparatus innovation were gone down through centuries, adding to the combined social achievements of human social organizations.

5. **Technological Development and Mental Complexity:**

The movement of instruments over the long haul echoes a direction of mechanical growth and growing mental complications. From uncomplicated handaxes to current sharp edges and in the long run to particular devices for diverse activities, the growth of apparatuses represented the expansion of mental powers. The advancement of composite equipment, such as lance hurlers and bows, needed specific knowledge as well as a more comprehensive grasp of material science and mechanics.

As technological innovation grew, so did the mental requirements of individuals. Complex machines needed more mind-boggling arranging, accurate execution, and an understanding of the connections between different elements. This pattern of mechanical progress and cerebral sophistication developed into a hallmark of human advancement, moving Homo sapiens into new areas of adaptability and success.

6. **Symbolic Portrayal and Language:**
The utilization of tools likewise assumed a critical job in the advancement of symbolic representation and language. Apparatuses become utilitarian devices as well as iconic augmentations of human vision. Early people used machines to ensure persistence as well as for symbolic articulation, including in traditions or artistic ventures.

The ability to develop and use instruments demanded an understanding of images and depiction. The interchange of knowledge regarding gadgets via language developed into a powerful mental tool, allowing more effective correspondence and coordinated effort within gatherings. The growth of language and symbolic depiction intermingled with instrument usage, spurring the development of sophisticated cerebral skills that placed mankind away from other animals.

7. **Cognitive Variations in Device Making:**
The demonstration of hardware creation itself went through conceptual changes. It needed a psychological depiction of the perfect instrument, an understanding of the unpolished components

available, and the ability to transform these materials into usable equipment. These mental cycles comprised working memory, scrupulousness, and the ability to organize and organize tasks.

After some time, when equipment-producing tactics came out to be more complex, so did the mental requirements. The development of distinct tools for specified undertakings requires a detailed knowledge of the atmosphere and the primary tasks. Mental alterations in gadget construction were a response to outside challenges as well as a primary stimulus in the growth of human knowledge.

Effect of Devices and Innovations: The utilization of devices and innovations addresses an augmentation of mental capabilities beyond the inherent imperatives of the mind. Darwinian points of view short us to study how the growth and authority of apparatuses have developed critical thinking skills, spatial understanding, and the capacity to manage the climate in methods that promote endurance and proliferation.

The relationship between equipment usage and mental progressions is woven into the real texture of human development. From the first rudimentary gadgets to the baffling improvements of today, the mental adventure of Homo sapiens has been fashioned by the requirement to produce and operate tools. Apparatus utilization represents down-to-earth critical thinking skills as well as social transmission, mechanical development, and the improvement of symbolic depiction. The mental differences linked with instrument usage stand as a manifestation of the significant knowledge of our species, demonstrating how the dominion of gadgets evolved into an incredible power that propelled humanity toward unparalleled mental achievements.

Chapter 4

Brain Evolution

4.1 Encephalization and Brain Size: Unraveling the Complexities of Cognitive Evolution**

The confusing link connecting encephalization and mind size is a basis for figuring out the evolution of mental boundaries throughout species. Encephalization, the overall size of the cerebrum contrasted with weight, has had a key influence on shaping the mental sceneries of numerous living beings. From the littlest vertebrates to the substantially encephalized human cerebrum, this mind-boggling interchange between mind size and mental capabilities displays the complexities of transforming cycles and the various rewards supplied by an expanded cerebrum.

1. **Defining Encephalization Remainder (EQ):**

Encephalization is assessed using the Encephalization Remainder (EQ), a measure that looks at the actual mind size of a creature to the usual cerebrum size given its weight. This percentage enables scientists to examine the amount of encephalization and offers insights into the mental capabilities of animal types.

While EQ is a major instrument, it's vital to take notice that mind size alone doesn't grasp the intricacies of mental talents. The connection and availability of brain organizations, as well as the individual variations of cerebrum districts, contribute fundamentally to the mental capacity of a creature.

2. **Evolutionary Patterns in Encephalization:**

Across evolutionary history, numerous animals have demonstrated patterns in encephalization. For instance, highly developed species, notably primates, display increased encephalization compared with diverse vertebrates. Inside the primate desire, individuals stand out with an exceptionally high EQ, displaying a lopsidedly enormous cerebrum comparable with body size.

The developmental direction of encephalization isn't universal. A few lineages exhibit expansions in EQ after some years, showing diverse responses to ecological problems and the benefits of better mental limitations. Conversely, some species could demonstrate declines in EQ due to unique strains leaning toward energy production or other flexible techniques.

3. **The Human Encephalization Story:**

Human encephalization covers a remarkable element in the developmental narrative. The human cerebrum, comprising roughly 2% of whole body weight, uses a lopsidedly large measure of metabolic energy, indicating the significance of mental skills in our species. The evolution of the human cerebrum is set apart by a large expansion in size and complexity, prompting the advent of cutting-edge mental skills like language, conceptual reasoning, and social understanding.

The expansion of the human cerebrum is considered to be associated with the obstacles given by our familial circumstances. As early primates adjusted to shifting biological circumstances, mental talents that worked with critical thinking, equipment usage, and social cooperation provided obvious rewards. The positive criticism loop between a developed mind improved mental capacities, and increased flexibility undoubtedly assumed a key role in the evolution of Homo sapiens.

4. **Factors Affecting Mind Size and Encephalization:**

A few aspects contribute to variances in mind size and encephalization between species:

a. **Ecological Pressures:** - Natural components, for example, the complexity of the environment and the problems it provides, affect the unique pressures pushing toward larger cerebrums. Species encountering varied biological needs could acquire larger cerebrums to truly investigate and adapt to their circumstances.

b. **Social Complexity:** - Species that engage in complex social relationships usually demonstrate increased encephalization. The requirements of keeping up with social progressive systems, recognizing individual collecting people, and discovering intricate social aspects could drive the development of larger cerebrums.

c. **Diet and Scavenging Strategies:** - The sort of food an animal typically adopts may impact cerebrum growth. For instance, animals with a more varied and demanding diet could grow larger brains to enhance innovative rummage skills, instrument usage, and critical thinking abilities.

d. **Life History Traits:** - Life history characteristics, including life duration and conceptive systems, extra assume a role. Species with longer life spans and more extended periods of dependence on acquiring could benefit from larger brains prepared for gathering and applying knowledge over the long run.

5. **Neurological Transformations and Cortical Expansion:**

The growth of an enlarged mind encompasses an increase in generally speaking size as well as clear neurobiological changes. Specifically, the expansion of the neocortex, the exterior layer of the cerebrum connected with better mental skills, is a critical component in the development of encephalization.

The neocortex in humans is lopsidedly big contrasted with different animals, specifically in parts linked with key skills, palpable management, and association regions. This cerebral expansion is associated with the enhancement of complicated mental skills, including language, unique reasoning, and critical thinking.

6. **Comparative Encephalization Across Species:**

While contrasting encephalization among animals, various examples arise:

a. **Primates:** - Among primates, humans have the most significant EQ. This is represented in the complexity of human cognition, including increased specialization, equipment utilization, and social cooperation. Different primates, like chimpanzees and dolphins, moreover demonstrate more substantial amounts of encephalization contrasted with non-primate well-developed organisms.

b. **Cetaceans:** - Cetaceans, especially dolphins and whales, are famous for their high encephalization comparable with body size. These oceanic highly developed organisms demonstrate complicated social methods of interacting,

contemporary communication, and vital capacities to think, emphasizing the relevance of an expanded mind in adapting to sea-going settings.

c. **Elephants:** - Elephants, are noted for their incredible memory and

critical thinking ability, and also demonstrate greater degrees of encephalization. Their social complexity and lengthy life spans contribute to the developmental stresses tending toward greater brains.

d. **Birds:** - While traditionally linked with more modest brains, several bird species, for example, corvids (e.g., crows and ravens) and

parrots, demonstrate improved mental powers and critical thinking skills. These birds have increased encephalization compared with other avian species.

7. **Limitations and Criticisms:**

While encephalization delivers considerable encounters into mental advancement, it has obstructions and challenged reactions:

a. **Neural Efficiency:** - Some believe that straightforward cerebrum size, as opposed to encephalization, could be a more precise predictor of mental skills. Species with more modest brains but better brain efficiency might demonstrate essentially equal mental capacities.

b. **Selective Pressures:** - The variables determining mind size and encephalization are confusing and interwoven. Specific stresses could follow up on numerous qualities all the while, making it challenging to establish a single fundamental impulse behind mental growth.

c. **Alternative Measures:** - A few experts offer chosen measurements, like the number of neurons or the complexity of brain relationships, as extra instructional indicators of mental talents. These behaviors could offer a more detailed grasp of the brain concept of insight.

The mind-boggling dance between cerebrum size, encephalization, and mental capacity exposes a complex patchwork of variations and changes throughout the tree of life. From the deeply encephalized human mind to the astounding mental boundaries of diverse animals, the progress of understanding reflects the unique exchange of science and climate. Encephalization, as a measurement, helps us to analyze and look at these variances, offering a window into the varied approaches by which biological creatures have investigated the intricate issues of their unique worlds.

As we carry on disentangling the mysteries of encephalization and mind growth, evidently insight is a complicated uniqueness. The progression of perception is not fully set in stone by the size of the mind nevertheless contains puzzling brain architecture, hierarchical instances, and the transaction of numerous unique tensions. By diving into the complexities of encephalization, we obtain a more thorough understanding of the numerous mental scenarios that have formed all through the transformational trip, each a manifestation of the enormous diversity and inventiveness of life on The planet.

4.2 Neurological Adaptations for Cognitive Complexity: Unraveling the Intricacies of Advanced Cognition**

The growth of cutting-edge mental capabilities in distinct animals is unexpectedly tied to neurological changes that empower complicated data management, critical thinking, and diverse methods of acting. From the unexpected brain groupings of the human cerebrum to the critical thinking abilities of particular creature species, these neurological differences emphasize the unique transaction involving science and perception. Understanding the various brain systems that operate with mental complexity offers insights into the astonishing range of mental capacities throughout the animals of the planet collectively.

1. **The Brain Engineering of Mental Complexity:**

At the root of mental complexity is the many-sided brain architecture that works with data management, learning, and direction. The cerebrum, a gigantically complex organ, is comprised of billions of neurons linked by neurotransmitters. The fundamental and beneficial linkage of these brain networks plays a vital role in choosing the mental capabilities of animal groupings.

In substantially encephalized creatures, for example, humans and some monkeys, the neocortex is a major player. This exterior layer of the mind is connected with higher mental talents, including tactile insight, spatial reasoning, language, and leadership capabilities. The growth and development of the neocortex contribute to the greater mental sophistication found in these animals.

2. **Enlarged Prefrontal Cortex: The Seat of Chief Functions:**

The prefrontal cortex, a region positioned in the front section of the mind, is notably vital for mental complexity. This area is linked with leader capacities, which encompass a variety of higher-request mental cycles, for example, autonomous direction, critical thinking, arranging, and restraint.

In individuals, the prefrontal cortex is extraordinarily evolved and includes a crucial element of the neocortex. The development of the prefrontal cortex is recognized to be a major neurological variation that has given high-level mental skills one of a kind to our animal kinds. The mind-baffling connections within this sector take into account the synchronization of data from distinct tangible modalities and the arrangement of difficult mental activities.

3. **Mirror Neurons and Social Cognition:**

Reflect neurons are another neurobiological oddity that contributes to mental complexity, particularly in the realm of social perception. Found in the macaque monkeys and subsequently worked on in humans, reflect neurons will be neurons that activate both when an individual performs an activity and when they perceive another person carrying out a comparable action.

These neurons assume a crucial position in interpreting and replicating the behaviors of others, establishing the cause for compassion, impersonation, and social learning. The existence of mirror neurons in some species, notably those with cutting-edge social designs, replicates a neurological difference that boosts their ability to study complicated social features.

4. **Hippocampus and Spatial Cognition:**

Spatial awareness, the ability to examine and mentally confront spatial situations, is a crucial aspect of mental complexity. The hippocampus, a seahorse-formed structure deep within the mind, is crucial to spatial learning and memory.

In animals that demonstrate advanced spatial vision, for example, some bird species and highly developed organisms, the hippocampus is typically amplified and practically particular. This metamorphosis enables these animals to build mental guides, examine difficult settings, and take part in methods of acting like rummaging and regional guard.

5. **Neuroplasticity and Learning:**

Brain adaptability, the mind's capability to remodel itself by forming new brain connections, is a fundamental neurobiological transition that underpins learning and memory. The limit concerning brain adaptability permits individuals to adjust to growing surroundings, learn new skills, and modify their behavior in light of engagement.

In animals with significant mental complexity, brain adaptability is typically articulated, contemplating the adaptable modification of brain circuits in light of ecological enhancements. This adaptability contributes to the learning and critical thinking talents observed in many organisms, from equipment-creating monkeys to critical-thinking cephalopods.

6. **Dopaminergic Frameworks and Prize-Based Learning:**

Dopaminergic frameworks, including the synapse dopamine, assume an essential role in recompense-based learning and inspiration. The expectancy and receipt of remunerations prompt the entrance of dopamine in the mind, creating methods of behavior connected with pleasant consequences.

In animals with cutting-edge mental capacities, the dopaminergic frameworks are highly tailored to enable complicated learning and dynamic cycles. This transition helps individuals assess the value of diverse actions, make projections regarding future consequences, and take part in objectively coordinated methods of acting.

7. **Communication Networks:**

In species with complicated correspondence frameworks, certain brain differences assist the handling and translation of open signals. The ability to interpret and generate multiple vocalizations, gestures, or diverse sorts of communication is typically related to certain brain areas.

For instance, in warblers, the unique brain circuits in the cerebrum encourage the learning and development of mind-boggling melodies. Essentially, in cetaceans like dolphins, many-sided communication frameworks are sustained by specialized cerebrum districts that function with the translation of vocalizations.

8. **Cognitive Compromises and Energy Costs:**

While cutting-edge mental capabilities give substantial rewards, there are compromises and energy expenditures linked with preserving a profoundly developed cerebrum. The cerebrum is a vigorously requiring organ, and species with enlarged mental complexity should designate greater assets to improve mind capacity.

The evolution of cutting-edge cognizance entails investigating these tradeoffs, and improving mental powers while settling the metabolic needs of an enlarged and energetically extravagant mind.

Species that efficiently cope with these tradeoffs display the flexible value of mental complexity in their various ecological specializations.

9. **Examples of Neurological Transformations in Species:**

a. **Cephalopods:** - Octopuses and squids, notwithstanding having decentralized sensory systems, demonstrate outstanding cerebral skills. The confusing connection of their large brains takes into account advanced critical thinking, learning, and the usage of tools. Their aptitude to camouflage and investigate difficult situations parallels the brain changes that aid their mental abilities.

b. **Tool-Utilizing animals:** - Apparatus utilizing animals, for example, chimpanzees and capuchin monkeys, show advanced critical thinking talents associated with unique brain variations. The observation, mimicry, and transmission of hardware usage methods of acting incorporate sophisticated brain circuitry, notably in regions linked with engine arranging and coordination.

c. **Birds of Prey:** - Flying predators, for example, hawks and birds, demonstrate improved spatial discrimination and accurate hunting strategies. Their cerebrums feature particular transformations, including evolved optic curves and visual handling habitats, which support their

extraordinary visual sharpness and ability to explore three-layered situations amid high-velocity elevated pursuits.

d. **Cetaceans:** - Dolphins, recognized for their mind-boggling connection, social designs, and critical thinking abilities, have big and substantially twisted cerebrums. The specialization of cerebrum districts, notably in the hear-able and echolocation focuses, works with their complicated connection and route under oceanic settings.

10. **Human Uniqueness and Brain Specializations:**

The outstanding mental complexity noticed in persons is associated with extraordinary brain specializations. The improvement of language, conceptual thinking, and social transmission contains diverse cooperations between numerous mind locations.

In the human mind, Broca's area and Wernicke's region, placed on the left side of the equator, are crucial for language processing. The prefrontal cortex, particularly the dorsolateral prefrontal cortex, is implicated in executive capacities and sophisticated critical thinking. These brain specializations contribute to the phenomenal mental skills that distinguish persons from various species

The neurological alterations for mental complexity address a compelling tapestry weaved through the development of

various species. From the unusually advanced human cerebrum to the astonishing mental achievements of various organisms, these modifications showcase the adaptability and versatility of brain structures because of ecological challenges.

As scientists keep on disentangling the complexity of neurobiology and mental growth, evidently developed perception isn't constrained to a single outline. All things being equal, many species have progressed unique neurological alterations custom-matched to their natural specializations, social designs, and flexible methods. The research of these alterations enhances how we can understand mental variation as well as reveals the monumental combos and divergences that shape the brain sceneries of living on The planet.

Chapter 5

Language Evolution

5.1 Origins of Language and Communication

Origins of Language and Communication: A Journey Through Human Evolution

The beginning points of language and communication address a major piece in the transformational narrative of Homo sapiens. As animal kinds, humans have cultivated a refined arrangement of communication that rises beyond the utilitarian trade of facts, including complicated etymological designs, symbolic depiction, and the ability to express intellectual contemplations. Disentangling the roots of language requires exploring the developmental, mental, and social aspects that formed this distinctive human ability.

1. Developmental Setting: From Primates to Homo sapiens

The basic underpinnings of language and correspondence may be traced back to our primate forefathers. While numerous animals demonstrate patterns of connection, the evolution of language in Homo sapiens addressed a subjective step. The move towards bipedalism, enlarged cerebrum size, and the improvement of a larynx equipped for making various sounds set up for the growth of etymological skills.

The evolution from Australopithecus to Homo, marked off by species like Homo habilis and Homo erectus, witnessed the gradual advancement of gadgets and social arrangements. Correspondence, at first relying on gestures, vocalizations, and possibly basic representational articulations, acquired a crucial role in coordinating bunch activities, communicating data about assets, and setting out friendly relationships.

2. Mental Establishments: The Cerebrum and Language Processing

The evolution of language is complicatedly tied to mental variations, notably in the architecture and capabilities of the mind. The neocortex, the exterior layer of the mind connected with higher mental capacity, went undergone significant growth in Homo sapiens. The specialized areas involved with language processing, such as Broca's region and Wernicke's region, showed brain modifications that operated with complicated etymological skills.

The development of a sophisticated working memory, attentional processes, and the ability to manage conceptual representations provided the mental basis for language. These alterations let early individuals transmit prompt concerns as well as take part in more distinctive reasoning, arrange for the future, and express intricate tales.

3. Social Elements: Collaboration, Trust, and Shared Intentions

Language and correspondence are inextricably interwoven with the social features of early human networks. The ability to communicate truly enhanced cooperation worked with common expectancies, and contributed to the expansion of trust within gatherings. Shared expectancies contain the ability to communicate about beneficial exercises, coordinate actions, and aggregate achieve goals.

Language, in its beginning structures, lets individuals transmit aims, express sentiments, and direct activities, for example, hunting or mutual asset collection. The increase of trust and similar aims within a local region supplied substantial rewards regarding endurance, asset procurement, and protection against outside threats.

4. Motions, Vocalizations, and Protolanguage: Antecedents to Speech

Before the advent of properly developed language, early humans presumably relied on an arrangement of protolanguage, incorporating signals, glances, and vocalizations. Gestural communication, notably, would play a vital role in passing on facts, conveying sentiments, and coordinating workouts.

The transition towards discourse involved the refinement and synchronization of vocalizations, aided by anatomical modifications like the lowered larynx. This regarded a more significant scope of sounds and enlarged vocal control, providing the basis for the diverse phonetic collection observed in current-day dialects. The coordination of signals and vocalizations in protolanguage presumably operated with more intricate and established subordinate connections.

5. Emblematic Portrayal: From Cement to Digest Concepts

The potential to incorporate visuals for communicating marked a great leap toward the evolution of language. Early individuals started applying graphics to address major things, actions, or concepts. Cave compositions, basic sketches, and symbolic antiquities recovered from archeological places testify to this representational depiction.

As mental skills grew, symbolic depiction stretched from extensive portrayals to extract concepts. The utilization of pictures took into consideration the communication of extra intricate concepts, the depiction of dynamic ideas, and the building of tales that extended beyond fast encounters. Emblematic representation emerged become a helpful tool for passing on facts about the world, social practices, and shared beliefs.

6. Social Development: Language as a Powerful System

Language isn't static yet goes through continual growth within human social hierarchies. Social transmission takes a crucial position in the course of events and the evolution of languages throughout millennia. As individuals impart, exchange tales, and interact within a local region, etymological components are depending upon diversity, growth, and transmission.

Social evolution influences not merely the jargon and punctuation of a language but also its nuances, sayings, and articulations. Various people groups promote distinct semantic features, prompting the rich diversity of dialects recognized worldwide. The flexibility of language as a unique framework helps it to conform to altering social, social, and ecological circumstances over the long term.

7. Device Use and Mental Headways: The Coevolution of Language

The coevolution of language and technological usage is an enthralling component of human growth. Instrument usage, which originated before the advent of totally developed language, affects the evolution of mental faculties and correspondence. The coordination anticipated for apparatus creation and instrument usage likely elaborate increased relational capacities, nurturing the expansion of further refined forms of language.

Alternately, the evolution of language worked with increasingly strong combined effort in gadget usage. The ability to pass on itemized data concerning apparatus development, hunting methods, and asset utilization via language increased the efficiency of collecting activities. This interchange among language and equipment use contributed to the result of Homo sapiens in adapting to various settings.

8. Natural Premise of Language: Qualities, FOXP2, and Beyond

Hereditary investigations have supplied insights into the natural basis of language. The FOXP2 quality, connected with language and discourse progression, went through developing adjustments in human heredity. While FOXP2 isn't the lone predictor of language skills, its role in brain improvement and discourse-related engine management underlines the hereditary commitments to phonetic boundaries.

Past clear attributes, the complex transaction of various hereditary variables, brain organizations, and ecological influences contribute to language acquisition and improvement. The multiple hereditary and cerebral basis of language underlines the deep mix of phonetic skills with the more substantial biological setting of human growth.

9. Developmental Benefits of Language: Variation and Survival

The improvement of language supplied crucial varied advantages to early human populaces. Compelling communication is considered to facilitate a lot of activities, shared direction, and cooperative critical thinking. The ability to pass on info about the environment, including projected hazards and assets, increased the endurance and conceptive result of individuals within gatherings.

Language likewise acquired a critical position in the advancement of social practices, the transfer of knowledge, and the creation of common characteristics. The sharing of data via language operated with the collecting of social understanding, technical breakthroughs, and flexible systems throughout centuries.

10. Present day Points of view: Mental Phonetics and Transformative Psychology

Present-day points of view on the genesis of language derive from mental phonetics and transformational brain research. Mental etymology explores the mental components of essential language usage, highlighting the role of mental representations, applied allegories, and characterized understanding. This method focuses on how language reflects and changes how individuals think and experience the world.

Developmental brain study attempts to understand the varied parts of mental traits, including language, by analyzing their transformational beginning places. It explores how mental and behavioral traits emerged to solve explicit issues in inherited disorders. The transformational point of view offers insights into the unique dynamics that produced the growth and improvement of language in human developmental history.

Disentangling the Embroidered Artwork of Human Communication**

The initial points of language and communication offer an exciting tour through the chronicles of human evolution. From the gesture and vocal articulations

Since our primate ancestors to the many-sided semantic tapestry created by contemporary-day humanity, language has been a dynamic and adaptable mechanism that has changed our mental picture.

The growth of language is certainly not a direct movement nevertheless a baffling combination of physiological, mental, social, and societal elements. It symbolizes the creativity of human diversity, the extravagance of our social inheritance, and the limit of language to ascend beyond the rapid and connect us to shared tales, collective knowledge, and the wide span of human experience.

As we go more into the complexity of language beginning points, we find the mechanics of communication as well as the content of what makes us incredibly human. It is a narrative inscribed in the neurotransmitters of our cerebrums, conveyed in the diversity of dialects spoken around the world and a demonstration of the persisting power of human connection via words.

5.2 Cognitive Implications of Linguistic Development: Navigating the Landscape of Human Thought**

The excursion of phonetic turn of events, from the establishment of vital correspondence in our transforming past to the many-sided dialects spoken now, is entangled with major mental consequences. Language isn't only a vehicle for connection; it fills in as a window into the depths of human vision, profoundly affecting viewpoints, key capacities to think, and the real texture of our psychological situations. This inquiry goes into the mental consequences of etymological turn of events, exposing the essential methods by which language molds and mimics the operations of the human brain.

1. Language as a Mental Device: Outlining Thought Processes

Language is more than a technique for expressing past ideas; it effectively impacts the method in which we believe. The Sapir-Whorf conjecture, commonly referred to as phonetic relativity, establishes that the language we capitalize on drives our mental cycles and even designs our picture of the globe. Various dialects provide distinct techniques for summarizing interactions, categorizing ideas, and conveying relationships between concepts.

For instance, languages with linguistic orientation, like Spanish or German, relegate orientation to objects. This phonetic factor alters how speakers view and understand things, pairing orientation explicit features with lifeless material. The emotional repercussions of such etymological highlights go far outside basic language designs, altering how individuals think and relate to their broad environment.

2. Language and Mental Adaptability: Adjusting to Perspectives

Multilingualism provides an enthralling focal point through which to study mental adaptability. People competent in several dialects typically exhibit an increased ability to switch between distinct thinking systems. This mental flexibility reaches out to critical thinking, imaginative reasoning, and adapting to different social contexts.

The approach connected with investigating many phonetic frameworks expects individuals to consistently flip between mental modes, a training that cultivates adaptability and a sophisticated appreciation of various social and etymological nuances. Multilingual persons display a better capacity to perceive conditions according to multiple views, a competence that may impact distinct sections of brain activity.

3. Language and Memory: Mental Aids and Mental Strategies

Language takes a significant position in remembering, coming in as a powerful mental assistant. The use of language to encode, store, and retrieve data increases memory upkeep. The construction of reports, word linkages, and etymological instances aids with organizing and combining memories.

As well as supporting memory preservation, language equally affects the mechanisms individuals employ to analyze and assess facts. The encoding of facts into words, whether spoken or created, enhances the profundity of managing and works with recuperation. The mental consequences go out beyond the fast presentation of communication, molding how individuals structure their contemplations and draw in their memories.

4. Language and Critical Thinking: The Job of Unique Thinking

Language is a medium for distinctive thinking, letting folks conceive and investigate concepts beyond prompt physical experiences. Unique notions, like love, equality, or a majority rules system, gain expression via language, permitting humans to battle with complicated thoughts that reach beyond actual reality.

The power to articulate and regulate conceptual concepts is an indication of cutting-edge mental functioning. Language supplies a platform to digest thinking, letting folks join in theoretical thinking, consider elective possibilities, and take care of situations that involve higher-request mental cycles. The mental repercussions of language in critical thinking underline its duty as a mental instrument for examining the complexity of human notions.

5. Metacognition and Language: Considering Thought Processes

Metacognition, the ability to screen and examine one's thought processes, follows down articulation via language. The explanation of concerns, intentions, and reflections allows individuals to take part in metacognitive activities. Language offers a mechanism to convey the content of concerns as well as the cycles of reasoning.

The use of language for metacognitive goals encompasses self-talk, internal exchanges, and explicit critical thinking methods. Through etymological articulation, individuals may externalize their concerns, making them available for reflection and scrutiny. This metacognitive aspect of language contributes to awareness, contemplation, and the potential to improve one's thinking cycles.

6. Language and Social Cognizance: Exploring Social Dynamics

The social aspect of language is crucial to figuring out its mental repercussions. Language isn't simply a way to supply unique opinions however in addition an instrument for examining intricate societal features. Discussions include the trade of data as well as the exchange of social jobs, progressive systems, and common norms.

The mental repercussions of language in friendly circumstances comprise the ability to interpret others' ideas, understand verified significant gestures, and engage in sophisticated forms of social reasoning. The intricacies of etymological articulation, including tone, pitch, and nonverbal cues, contribute to the complex tapestry of social awareness. The enhancement of the hypothesis of the brain, the ability to credit mental states to oneself as well as other individuals, is tightly entangled with the etymological turn of events and its social repercussions.

7. Language Securing and Mental Turn of Events: Early Foundations

The mental excursion begins with language securing throughout youth, signifying a vital period in mental turn of events. The most usual approach to learning language contains complicated mental tasks, including design acknowledgment, familiar learning, and the capacity to sum up semantic standards. Babies have an inborn restriction about language acquisition, demonstrating a preference for processing semantic data and deleting crucial instances.

As children advance via language improvement successes, their cerebral skills increase. The gaining of grammar, jargon, and linguistic designs contains the refining of mental cycles linked with recall, consideration, and critical thinking. Language procurement fills in as a vital step in the mental turn of events, establishing the basis for more developed mental capacities in subsequent stages of life.

8. Brain adaptability and Language Getting the hang of Adjusting Brain Networks

The mental repercussions of language stretch out to the brain adaptability witnessed during language acquisition. The cerebrum demonstrates remarkable adaptability because of phonetic contribution, with brain networks reorganizing to oblige new linguistic skills. This adaptability is notably expressed in adolescence however carry on into maturity, letting folks obtain new languages all of their life.

The mental cycles connected with language acquisition comprise hearable segregation, design acknowledgment, and the enhancement of phonetic responsiveness. The commitment of these mental resources reshapes brain connections, highlighting the bidirectional relationship between language and mental functioning. The pliancy seen in language acquisition illustrates the tremendous interaction between the etymological turn of events and mental alteration.

9. Language and Mental Deterioration: Suggestions for Aging

The mental consequences of language go out over life expectancy, with language taking a role in easing mental degeneration in later years. Bilingualism, for example, has been connected with mental hold, prolonging the starting old enough related mental degeneration. The continual mental commitment necessary for coping with distinct languages is considered to contribute to the conservation of mental capabilities.

Also, fascinating in semantic activities, like perusing, creating, or acquiring new dialects, has been related to mental imperativeness in more seasoned grown-ups. The continued utilization of language, alongside the mental asks it involves, helps to keep up with cerebral capacity and power against age-related deterioration.

10. Innovative Advances and Mental Expansions: From Writing to Computerized Communication

The evolution of correspondence advancements has broadened the mental scene linked with language. Composing, as an externalized sort of language, takes into consideration the conservation and diffusion of knowledge over eras. The appearance of printing also elevated the mental consequences of written language, democratizing access to info and boosting academic progressions.

In the advanced era, technological apparatuses, for example, mobile phones and the web have modified the approaches by which we draw in with language. The cerebral repercussions of electronic communication encompass quick data management, executing numerous jobs, and the synchronization of sight and hearing components. The innovative notion of automated communication phases gives extra options for semantic

Chapter 6

Social Cognition

6.1 Evolutionary Roots of Social Intelligence: Navigating the Tapestry of Social Interaction**

The transforming effects of participation are evident in the diverse results of animals that engage in cooperative methods of behavior. Agreeable living increases the ability to take benefit of diverse environmental specializations, defend from hunters, and access assets that would be challenging for lone individuals. The growth of assemblages affords a cradle against ecological weaknesses and increases the robustness of species after some time.

In individuals, the upsides of participation stretch out to the social domain, where cooperative endeavors lead to mechanical innovations, logical headways, and the improvement of challenging social systems. The restriction with regards to social transmission takes into consideration the gathering of knowledge and varied approaches over ages, further adding to the result of human pleasant endeavors.

10. Difficulties to Participation: Contest and Cheating

While cooperation provides different rewards, issues likewise develop in keeping up with helpful frameworks. Rivalry for assets, irreconcilable scenarios, and the potential for individuals to take advantage of pleasant frameworks via conning give continual challenges to the solidity of societal

gatherings.

In diverse animals, strategies have emerged to solve these issues. Discipline of miscreants, societal authorizations, and components for identifying and prohibiting non-cooperators contribute to the support of agreeable frameworks. The transaction between cooperation and contest generates dynamic social scenes where the harmony among individual and collective interests determines the evolutionary direction of species.

The Woven Artwork of Agreeable Existence**

A helpful style of acting and general sentiments build a complex needlework that crosses the expansiveness of transforming history. From the minute cooperation of tiny creatures to the unanticipated societal designs of people, the numerous techniques produced out of cooperative effort have shaped the direction of existence on the planet. The examination of helpful styles of acting enlightens the power, adaptability, and ingenuity imprinted in the convoluted web of social communications across distinct animals.

Participation continues as a show of the power of aggregate undertakings in beating problems, upgrading asset usage, and creating versatile advancement. Whether through complex flags, sophisticated motions, vocalizations, or language, correspondence fills in as the cord that links people within gatherings. The instruments of communication, charity, and compromise further increase the security of agreeable frameworks.

As we contemplate the subtleties of helpful methods of acting and overall feelings, we get insights into the delicate harmony of individual and collective interests that determines the growth of social species. It is a demonstration of the tremendous interconnectivity of life, where cooperation occurs as a basis of presence, fostering strength, progress, and the shared adventure of diverse animals through the needlework of time.

6.2 Cooperative Behavior and Group Dynamics: Exploring the Power of Collaboration"

Agreeable Way of acting and Collective vibes: Investigating the Force of Collaboration Agreeable manners of behaving and general feelings address significant elements of human cooperation, shaping societal designs, fostering aggregate successes, and impacting individual and aggregate prosperity. This inquiry looks into the subtleties of helpful manner of acting and general vibes, looking at their value in inspiring combined effort, developing cultural unification, and pushing human growth.

1. **Foundations of Helpful Behavior**

A helpful manner of acting, formed in the inherent sociality of individuals, envelops acts that concentrate on collective aims above individual interests. From early human social systems to contemporary-day advances, cooperation has been vital for survival, permitting individuals to pool assets, exchange knowledge, and work together toward typical aims. The developmental underlying foundations of helpful behavior are in the advantages it provides regarding asset security, assurance against hazards, and the aid of social ties.

2. **'The Elements of Gathering Interaction**

Overall vibes represent the complex interplay of individual individuals, influences, and ways of functioning within an aggregate context. As individuals meet together in meetings, they investigate components, for example, administration, communication designs, recognized norms, and dynamic cycles. Understanding collective vibes comprises examining how these components affect attachment, cooperation, and compromise within the gathering, subsequently molding its viability and efficiency.

3. **Benefits of Cooperation**

Helpful action delivers a plethora of benefits at both individual and collective levels. Exclusively, engagement develops social relationships, fabricates trust, and increases prosperity by meeting basic human requirements for belongingness and alliance. All in all, involvement enables gatherings to achieve outcomes that outshine the capacities of individuals alone, using varied skills, points of view, and assets to manage intricate challenges and search for common goals.

4. Promoting Social Union and Solidarity**

Helpful behavior fills in as a basis of social unity, fostering a sense of fortitude and connectivity within networks and social hierarchies. By fostering compassion, communication, and mutual support, participation fortifies social relationships, mitigates social solitude, and fosters a common sense of having a place. Amid the struggle, pleasant networks display flexibility, drawing from collective assets and strength to examine challenges and rebuild.

5. **Influences on Choice Making**

Overall vibes significantly alter dynamic cycles within groupings. From agreement to compromise, the characteristics of cooperation and contest impact how decisions are made and performed within meetings. Compelling dynamics rely on variables, for example, communication viability, administration approaches, and the capability to tolerate differing opinions while keeping up with group unity.

6. **Cultural Varieties in Cooperation**

Agreeable behavior displays itself uniquely throughout civilizations, indicating differences in acceptable norms, ideals, and genuine contexts. A few communities emphasize collective prosperity and connection, establishing strong mutual relationships and cooperative activities. Interestingly, others could stress individual independence and competitiveness, generating alternative articulations of partnership and overall emotions. Understanding social differences in participation enhances our passion for diversity and reveals ways for a multidimensional coordinated effort.

7. Challenges and Hindrances to Cooperation

Regardless of its inborn benefits, participation confronts obstacles and restrictions that might hamper its sustainability. These may involve challenges including competition for assets, irreconcilable conditions, dissimilar ambitions, and disruptions in communication. Conquering these issues takes intentional attempts to encourage trust, spell out clear norms and assumptions, and build open channels of connection within gatherings.

8. **The Job of Authority in Working with Cooperation**

Administration plays a vital role in dealing with partnerships and shaping collective sentiments. Powerful pioneers encourage trust, enhance inclusion, and develop a shared sense of purpose among different people. They influence their effect to invigorate joint effort, mediate conflicts, and engage folks to give their innovative assets to the aggregate undertaking. Initiative methods that stress straightforwardness, compassion, and participative dynamics usually foster a culture of cooperation within meetings.

9. **Applications in Different Contexts**

Agreeable methods of behaving and general feelings track down uses throughout various contexts, including company, training, medical services, and local area expansion. In corporate contexts, cooperative organizations accelerate progress, increase efficiency, and react to changing economic realities. In school, helpful learning techniques enhance understudy dedication, decisive reasoning, and friend support. In medical services, multidisciplinary groups coordinate consideration, work on quiet outcomes, and solve difficult wellness concerns.

10. **The Fate of Collaboration in a Globalized World**

As the globe comes out to be increasingly interrelated, participation anticipates more important relevance in responding to global issues, for example, environmental change, neediness, and pandemics. By embracing the norms of participation, fortitude, and shared responsibility, governments, groups, and networks may create cooperative arrangements that soar beyond geographical constraints and socioeconomic disparities. The ultimate destiny of participation consists of establishing comprehensive groups, applying aggregate wisdom, and saddling the power of combined effort to generate an extra-unbiased and maintainable planet.

All in all, pleasant methods of behaving and overall vibes address vital parts of human sociality, shaping cooperation, encouraging joint effort, and pushing aggregate development. By comprehending the aspects of participation and building a culture of cooperative effort, individuals and networks may face the force of collective action to solve issues, create flexibility, and produce a more hopeful time to come for a long time into the future.

Chapter 7

Technological Influences

7.1 Cognitive Evolution in the Context of Technological Advancements

Cognitive Evolution in the Context of Technological Advancements: Navigating the Frontiers of the Mind

The scene of human understanding has gone through exceptional adjustments combined with the determined trek of technological headways. From the early advances of constructed language to the sophisticated calculations of computerized reasoning, innovation has gone about as an incentive for mental evolution, transforming the method in which we think, learn, and cooperate with the world. This research digs into the relationship between mental development and innovative innovation, following the direction from crude mental capacities to the complexities of present psyche-machine interfaces.

1. The Composed Word: From Oral Custom to Literary Cognition

The arrival of composed language signified a key second in mental growth. As social systems evolved from oral practices to set down accounts, the human brain experienced new mental challenges. The power to encode facts written down externalized brain cycles, making ready for increased memory, communication, and the preservation of knowledge throughout ages.

The mental change linked with the created word comprised the gaining of education skills as well as the improvement of conceptual reasoning and the ability to investigate complicated data structures. The composed term went about as an exterior memory aid, releasing mental assets for higher-request mental talents like basic inquiry and creative amalgamation. The cerebral progress spurred by the prepared language set the groundwork for following technological advancements.

2. Print machine: Democratizing Information and Mental Impact

The introduction of the print machine in the fifteenth century heralded another age of mental improvement. The large-scale manufacture of books enabled the diffusion of knowledge to an unusual degree, democratizing admission to data and encouraging scholastic progressions. The cerebral repercussions of the print machine stretched to the formation of conclusive thin thinking individuals drawn in with varied points of view and concepts.

The capability to consume information from printed materials contributed to the development of logical skills and enhanced mental flexibility. Perusers were introduced to a broadness of issues, renewing scholastic curiosity and widening the mental skylines of individuals. The mental advancement worked with by the print machine set up for the Edification and the logical transformation, shaping the direction of human concepts.

3. Modern Upset: Mental Changes in Light of Mechanization

The Modern Unrest accomplished radical modifications in the economical and social texture of social systems, generating contrasting adjustments in mental requirements. Motorization and the rise of contemporary advancements modified workplaces, necessitating new mental qualities like errand proficiency, coordination, and flexibility to machine-driven procedures.

The mental development amid the Modern Transformation incorporated the integration of innovative apparatuses into day-to-day existence, anticipating humans to investigate increasingly baffling and computerized frameworks. The ability to understand and cooperate with hardware evolved into a major mental skill, duplicating the suppleness of the human brain to mechanical progressions in the working environment.

4. Electronic Correspondence: The Telecom Revolution

The nineteenth and twentieth hundreds of years witnessed the advent of electronic communication, marking one more triumph in mental progress. Broadcasts, phones, and later, the web, transformed how data was transmitted and obtained. The mental requirements linked with speedy communication and data access modified skills to concentration, performing multiple tasks capabilities, and the capacity to process vast quantities of knowledge.

The integrated notion of electronic communication nurtured a global exchange of ideas, societies, and data. People gained new mental capacities related to sorting and combining info from multiple sources. The mental growth because of internet communication emphasized the adaptability of the human psyche in adapting to the obstacles offered by progressing improvements.

5. Computerized Age: Data Over-burden and Mental Adaptations

The emergence of the advanced era took with it amazing admission to data however also the challenge of data over-burden. The sheer amount and rapid pace of data diffusion in the computerized realm demanded mental alterations to channel, assess validity and focus essential bits of knowledge from the vast ocean of information.

Mental development in the computerized era comprises the building of data proficiency capacities, decisive thinking, and the capacity to distinguish appropriate data in the middle of the tumult. The advanced scene also led to new sorts of mental commitment, including interactive media, intuitive substance, and the expansion of web networks. The growing mental requirements reflect the unique interplay between human understanding and the data-rich atmosphere of computerized time.

6. Computerized Reasoning: Coevolution of Machines and Minds

The integration of computerized thinking (simulated intelligence) into diverse characteristics of day-to-day living addresses a shift in viewpoint in mental growth. AI computations, normal language handling, and brain networks contribute to the development of insightful frameworks that can do complicated mental endeavors. The coevolution of humans and simulated intelligence improvements brings up difficulties concerning the development of mental capabilities and the moral contemplations enclosing human-machine affiliations.

Mental progression in the time of man-made intelligence contains the improvement of skills linked with combined effort with canny frameworks, comprehending algorithmic cycles, and adapting to the shifting scene of a company molded via robotization. The expansion of human discernment via artificial intelligence devices, such as language interpretation, image acknowledgment, and information examination, mimics the synergistic link between human personalities and machine insight.

7. Increased and Augmented Reality: Extending Perceptual and Mental Boundaries

The emergence of enhanced reality (AR) and computer-produced reality (VR) advancements acquaints new elements with mental development. These vivid inventions present unique means of meeting and engaging with material, questioning standard methods of understanding and awareness. The blend of AR and VR into industries like training, medical treatment, and diversion enhances the options for mental commitment and learning.

Mental alterations in light of extended and computer-created realities include spatial awareness, sensorimotor capacities, and the potential to explore virtual situations. The convergence of physical and electronic realms needs people to build mental adaptability and flexibility to replace ways of the actual world. The exploration of AR and VR addresses an area in mental growth, pushing the frontiers of how we view and engage with the environment.

8. Neurotechnologies: Testing the Boondocks of Mental Enhancement

Headways in neurotechnologies, like cerebrum PC connections and neurofeedback gadgets, provide the possibility for direct interactions between the human mind and outside gadgets. These advances raise moral contemplations, but in addition, they create roadways for mental improvement, neurorehabilitation, and the examination of the brain bases of discernment.

Mental development with regards to neurotechnologies comprises the improvement of brain adaptability and the capacity of the mind to modify and redesign in light of exterior upgrades. Mind-machine interfaces challenge traditional beliefs about mental constraints, permitting humans to control outside equipment or transmit via direct brain connections. The moral repercussions of mental expansion via neurotechnologies emphasize the demand for careful thinking about the influence on private personalities and cultural designs.

9. Deep-rooted Learning in the Information Economy: Constant Mental Adaptation

In the information economy, indicated by fast mechanical progressions and expanding expertise demands, long-lasting learning has changed into a cornerstone of mental advancement. The ability to gain new knowledge, upskill, and adapt to shifting competent scenes is key for investigating the problems of the cutting-edge labor force.

Mental growth in the information economy comprises the development of metacognitive capacities, autonomous learning, and computerized expertise. People should encourage the capacity to progress independently, fundamentally appraise data, and apply knowledge across multiple circumstances. The need for ongoing learning matches the strong notion of cerebral expansion in light of the constantly shifting mechanical environment.

10. Moral Contemplations: Exploring the Mental Outskirts Responsibly

As mental growth entwines with creative progressions, moral contemplations become primary. Questions encompassing protection, information security, predisposition in simulated intelligence computations, and the influence of innovation on emotional well-being highlight the necessity for competent growth. Mental development about innovation demands careful balance amid development and moral contemplations to secure the welfare of individuals and society at large.

Charting the Course of Cognitive Evolution**

The excursion of mental growth about creative headways is a unique narrative that unfurls at the crossing point of human creativity and the gradually rising boondocks of innovation. From the composed word to man-made awareness, each technological leap has created a lasting impression on the mental scene, defining the method in which we think, learn, and interact with the world.

The pliability of the human brain, displayed via mental transformations to technological developments, shows the diversity and flexibility of mental cycles. As we explore the mental fringes symbolizing things to come, the skillful reconciliation of innovation into our lives needs incisive contemplation of moral repercussions, cultural influence, and the conservation of key human traits.

Mental development, propelled by the driving power of creative innovation, urges us to accept the problems and open doors that lie ahead. In charting the trajectory of mental growth, we depart on an adventure of research, revelation, and continual variety, investigating the multidimensional interchange of brains and computers in the unfurling tale of human cognition.

7.2 Impact of Tools and Technologies on Human Cognition: From Stone Tools to Digital Frontiers**

The relationship between tools, inventions, and human cognition is a unique exchange that has sculpted the path of our species across the whole course of time. From the earliest stone tools to the intricacy of present technological innovations, every development has created a lasting stamp on the method by which we think, issue resolve, and cooperate with the globe. This examination dives into the important influence of instruments and innovations on human cognizance, following the developmental excursion that has unfurled at the confluence of creation and the brain.

1. Stone Instruments and Mental Precursors

The introduction of stone technologies signifies a critical crossroads in human evolution, reflecting the advent of mental powers new to our species. The manufacturing of devices demanded organizing, coordination, and the ability to handle unrefined ingredients, demonstrating an early sort of critical thinking and physical expertise. The usage of apparatuses not only increased endurance by assisting with hunting and processing food but also established the framework for the expansion of additional current mental capacities.

The mental influence of stone devices spread out beyond basic toolmaking skills. The skill to conceive and build gadgets provided a mental leap, permitting our progenitors to adapt to varied settings and demonstrate a degree of prescience in their actions. The relationship between instrument usage and mental enhancement developed into a marker of human development, providing room for subsequent progressions.

2. Horticultural Transformation: Instruments, Perception, and Social Complexity

The move from rural methods of living to horticulture marked a substantial change in human cognition. Agrarian devices, like furrows and sickles, revolutionized food generation and capability. The mental needs linked with horticulture included planning establishing seasons, managing assets, and working out the complexity of development.

The agricultural transition transformed resource systems as well as provide the framework for social complications. The management of larger scope cultivating networks demanded authoritative skills, communication, and the development of social progressive systems. Devices become expansions of real capabilities as well as impetuses for the growth of mental functions linked with collaboration, asset the board, and the coordination of aggregate efforts.

3. Composed Language: Instruments of Correspondence and Knowledge

The evolution of constructed language remains possibly one of the most astonishing devices in mankind's collection of experiences. The ability to address language emblematically empowered the capacity and conveyance of info throughout existence. The mental influence of prepared language was important, encouraging the growth of education skills, conceptual thinking, and the conservation of social knowledge.

Composed language evolved into a mental apparatus that ascended beyond individual memory, contemplating the gathering of knowledge beyond the range of oral conventions. The mental cycles linked with perusing and creating drew in locations of the cerebrum connected with pondering, decisive reasoning, and the combination of difficult notions. Composed language changed into a platform for higher-request mental capacities, working with headways in science, reasoning, and human expression.

4. Print machine: Instruments for Mass Correspondence and Information Dissemination

The invention of the print machine in the fourteenth century disturbed the transmission of knowledge. Printed books collaborated with the big-scale manufacture and dissemination of information, democratizing admission to training and writing. The mental influence of the print machine was dual; it increased proficiency rates and modified how people drew in with info.

The mental development linked with the print machine comprised the improvement of fundamental comprehension skills, logical thinking, and openness to various points of view. As books came out to be more open, individuals may research a broadness of issues, leading to the growth of academic interest and the expansion of mental skylines. The print machine set the groundwork for the Edification and the Logical Unrest, creating the mental picture of subsequent hundreds of years.

5. Modern Insurgency: Automation, Discernment, and Labor Force Shifts

The Modern Insurgency accomplished an inflow of mechanical advances that transformed assembly methods and the notion of labor. Hardware and equipment operated by steam and subsequently power affected the mental requirements of labor. Laborers are expected to adjust to machine-driven processes, requiring new mental abilities connected with task proficiency, coordination, and critical thinking in automated conditions.

The mental consequence of the Modern Transformation reached out to the management and association of vast-scope modern operations. The improvement of sequential building systems and creation frameworks needed mental skills linked with operations, asset identification, and the management of puzzling work procedures. The mental evolution during this century paralleled the flexibility of the human brain to the shifting landscape of innovation-driven labor.

6. Electronic Specialized: Devices for Worldwide Connectivity

The nineteenth and twentieth hundreds of years witnessed the emergence of electronic specialized devices, including broadcasts, phones, and finally the web. These innovations revolutionized how data was conveyed, connecting individuals over huge distances. The mental influence of electronic communication includes adapting to speedy data commerce, executing diverse jobs, and processing data in a worldwide linked atmosphere.

Electronic specialized equipment modified mental talents related to capacities to concentrate, data recovery, and the ability to investigate complicated structures of data. People gained new mental talents for sorting and integrating data from diverse sources, leading to the improvement of data education. The interrelated notion of electronic communication promoted worldwide commerce of ideas, societies, and data, altering mental points of view on a more expanded scale.

7. Advanced Age: Devices, Innovations, and Data Overload

The beginning of the electronic era provided another period of technology and developments with enormous repercussions for human perception. PCs, mobile phones, and the web become ubiquitous gadgets, modifying how individuals access, process, and produce data. The mental influence of the advanced era is shown by the test of data over-burden and the necessity to investigate an unquestionably sophisticated digital environment.

Mental transformations in the advanced age involve the growth of computerized instruction, decisive reasoning in evaluating web data, and the capacity to govern attention in an environment rich with boosts. The utilization of computerized equipment for correspondence, collaborative effort, and data recovery has become vital to day-to-day existence, shaping mental cycles linked with critical thinking, creativity, and social connection.

8. Computerized reasoning: Comprehension and Coordinated effort with Machines

The integration of computerized thinking (computer-based intelligence) into many elements of day-to-day living addresses a shift in viewpoint in human vision. AI computations, regular language handling, and insightful frameworks contribute to the improvement of machines that can do complicated mental assignments. The mental impact of simulated intelligence involves responding to a coordinated effort with sophisticated frameworks, comprehending algorithmic cycles, and experiencing a setting where machine insight complements human knowledge.

Computer-based intelligence instruments, from language interpretation to picture acknowledgment, extend human powers and reframe the bounds of mental chores. The mental growth in the period of simulated intelligence challenges usual conceptions of critical thinking and direction, highlighting a synergistic relationship between human personalities and computer knowledge. The moral contemplations including simulated intelligence further stress the demand for deliberate reconciliation into mental cycles.

9. Expanded and Augmented Reality: Devices for Perceptual Enhancement

The growth of enhanced reality (AR) and computer-produced reality (VR) advancements acquaints new elements with human perception. These vivid devices supply innovative ways to encounter and interact with facts, questioning usual techniques of discernment and awareness. The inclusion of AR and VR into many professions improves the potential for mental commitment, learning, and critical thinking..

Mental modifications due to enlarged and augmented realities include spatial discernment, sensorimotor skills, and the ability to explore and interact within virtual situations. These apparatuses increase perceptual experiences, delivering remarkable open doors for preparing, schooling, and reenactment. The mental influence of expanded and computer-produced reality goes beyond entertainment, contributing to progressions in domains like medicine, education, and planning.

10. Neurotechnologies: Devices for Testing and Upgrading Cognition

Headways in neurotechnologies include cerebrum PC interfaces and neurofeedback gear

, provide tools to manage connections between the human cerebrum and exterior technologies. These improvements create moral contemplations but in addition offer roadways for mental upgrading, neurorehabilitation, and the examination of the brain foundations of perception.

The mental influence of neurotechnologies comprises adapting to new methods of connection, for example, operating exterior gadgets by mind signals or taking part in neurofeedback to increase mental capabilities. These gadgets give pieces of understanding into the intricacies of brain cycles and provide open doors for customized intercessions to boost mental capabilities. The moral consequences of mental expansion via neurotechnologies highlight the delicate equilibrium between progress and competent utilization.

The Coevolution of Devices and Cognition**

The influence of gadgets and advances on human perception is an account of coevolution, where every development molds and is molded by the mental scene of our species. From the early utilization of stone apparatuses to the subtleties of computerized outside, gadgets have widened our real skills as well as have been critical to the method in which we think, study, and team up.

The mental alterations linked with instruments reflect the extraordinary flexibility and plasticity of the human brain. As we continue to expand and study new boondocks of innovation, the link among instruments and awareness will without a sure grow. The thoughtful incorporation of technology into our mental cycles involves ongoing thinking of moral consequences, cultural influence, and the safeguarding of important human attributes.

In studying the puzzling transaction involving gadgets and understanding, we depart on an excursion of disclosure, exposing the possibilities for extra progressions and modifying the real texture of human concepts. The coevolution of apparatuses and insight continues unfurling, encouraging us to examine the countless possible consequences that lie at the intersection of development and the brain.

Chapter 8

Cultural Evolution

8.1 Transmission of Knowledge and Cultural Impact on Cognition

Transmission of Information and Social Effect on Cognizance: The Embroidered Artwork of Shared Wisdom

The transmission of knowledge and the social milieu wherein it unfurls have substantial repercussions for the mental scene of persons and social orders. From oral traditions to the digital era, how knowledge is handed down affects mental cycles, affects critical thinking comes closer, and contributes to the development of individual and aggregate personalities. This inquiry goes into the delicate interchange between the transmission of information and social influence on perception, tracing the threads of shared astuteness that weave the woven artwork of human thought.

1. Oral Practices: Narrating and Mental Imprints

In the initial stages of mankind's collection of experiences, oral practices filled in as the primary means for transmitting knowledge starting with one age then onto the next. The specialization of telling, delivered by the stated word, took a focal role in shaping mental cycles. Accounts, tales, and social narratives handed down by oral practices not only maintained vital facts regarding survival, regular characteristics, and cultural norms however in addition left mental imprints on audience members.

The mental influence of oral traditions included the increase of memory capacities, as individuals needed to keep and examine massive measures of info supplied via tales. Moreover, the close-to-home and original aspects of telling drew in mental cycles related to compassion, creativity, and dynamic thinking. Oral customs created the basis for common social accounts that altered belief frameworks, social designs, and individual viewpoints.

2. Composed Language: Systematizing Information and Mental Expansion

The creation of constructed language marked a breakthrough step in the communication of information. The skill to address language emblematically enabled the keeping and conservation of facts written down. The mental influence of created language comprised the increase of education skills as well as the expansion of mental limitations linked with decisive thinking, inquiry, and contemplation.

The constructed word dealt with the codification of information, considering the production of texts, writing, and instructional resources. The cerebral cycles linked with perusing and creating pulled in higher-request thinking skills, boosting academic turn of events and the inquiry of different issues. The composed language developed became a medium for delivering down-to-earth facts as well as distinctive thoughts, altering the mental scene of individuals within educated cultures.

3. Print machine: Mass Scattering and Mental Revolution

The invention of the print machine in the fifteenth century revolutionized the distribution of knowledge. Printed books enabled wide-scale production, making data all the more broadly exposed. The mental influence of the print machine was complicated - it enlarged schooling rates, extended admission to a new scope of thinking, and contributed to a mental insurgency that affected the Renaissance and the Edification.

People were subjected to a more broad exposition of points of view, developing conclusive thinking and intellectual curiosity. The mental growth linked with the print machine included adapting to the enlarged data stream, building perceptive skills, and drawing in with a swiftly expanding group of facts. The democratization of data via printed materials set the basis for the cutting-edge moment of information communication.

4. Instructive Organizations: Formalizing Information and Mental Development

The construction of instructional organizations further structured the conveyance of information, formalizing the technique associated with learning. Schools, universities, and foundations became major experts in influencing mental turn of events. The mental influence of formal education contained the growth of exact thinking, logical talents, and the acquisition of special knowledge within clear disciplines.

Instructive institutions supplied an orderly framework for the transmission of social traits, logical norms, and cultural standards. The mental cycles connected with formal learning comprised the getting of verified material as well as the growth of decisive reasoning, critical thinking, and social discernment. Schooling systems were crucial to the social transfer of knowledge, impacting mental structures on both individual and societal levels.

5. Advanced Age: Information in the Data Age

The arrival of the computerized era has created another period of information transmission illustrated by the web, sophisticated media, and online stages. Data is presently spread at a spectacular pace, altering the method by which individuals access, exchange, and contribute information. The mental influence of the computerized era includes adapting to the speedy development of info, developing enhanced instruction, and experiencing a huge and linked computerized scene.

Online stages operate as focal places for the swapping of ideas, cooperative learning, and the development of virtual networks. The mental progression in the computerized era envelops skills linked with data recovery, fundamental evaluation of online content, and the ability to draw in various views. The democratization of knowledge via digital processes socially impacts judgment.

6. Social Accounts: Forming Personality and Worldviews

Social tales, implanted in dreams, literature, and verifiable records, play a vital role in creating individual and collective personalities. The transmission of social tales affects mental cycles related to self-insight, having a place, and the formation of viewpoints. Social tales go about as frameworks by which individuals comprehend their interactions and grasp their position within the more extended cultural context.

The mental influence of social storytelling involves the absorption of common values, norms, and belief frameworks. These tales contribute to the organization of social character, producing deep responses, moral contemplations, and dynamic cycles. The transmission of social tales across centuries generates a mental coherence that binds networks and contributes to the power of social heritage.

7. Language and Thought: Semantic Relativity and Mental Diversity

The relationship of language and cognition has been a matter of insightful desire, motivating the development of etymological relativity theories. These hypotheses claim that language affects mental cycles and changes the method by which individuals experience and arrange the world. The mental influence of linguistic variation is visible in the altering of applied structures, mental styles, and critical thinking techniques across distinct semantic networks.

societal transmission via language communicates explicit facts as well as inserts inferred societal norms and perspectives. The mental modifications linked with phonetic variation include the adaptability to study numerous etymological designs, the capability to switch between social casings of reference, and an awareness of the rich embroidered artwork of mental variety that semantic differences convey.

8. Native Information Frameworks: Conventional Insight and Mental Ecology

Native information frameworks, founded in the deep grasp of neighborhood biological systems and passed down through centuries, address outstanding storehouses of shrewdness. The transmission of local knowledge incorporates an all-encompassing manner to deal with the awareness that combines biological mindfulness, maintainability rehearses, and a substantial connection with the normal universe. The mental influence of native information frameworks stretches out beyond functional experiences to encompass a worldview that values connectivity, correspondence, and congruity with the climate.

The transfer of native knowledge comprises experience learning, oral conventions, and stereotyped rehearses. The mental variances connected with native information frameworks include a comprehensive biological understanding, responsiveness to occasional cycles, and a complex awareness of the relationships among persons and their regular environmental components. These information frameworks underline the relevance of multiple mental ecologies in the embroidered artwork of human perception.

9. Mechanical Education: Exploring the Computerized Frontier

In the electronic era, mechanical education has developed into a crucial aspect of information transmission. The ability to investigate advanced stages, fundamentally appraise online info, and draw in with coming innovations molds mental cycles in the current environment. The mental influence of mechanical education involves adapting to swiftly growing apparatuses, mastering complex interfaces, and taking part in the construction and dispersal of online substances.

Mechanical education likewise influences mental points of view on data authority, dependability, and the features of Internet networks. The transmission of information in the advanced outskirts incorporates the procurement of data as well as the expansion of skills linked with computerized correspondence, cooperative innovations, and moral contemplations in the web-based domain.

###** 10 Interdisciplinary Information: Integrating Points of View for Complex Challenges**

As information turns out to be increasingly specialized, there is a rising awareness of the value of multidisciplinary approaches. The transmission of transdisciplinary information comprises coordinating pieces of knowledge from various domains to meet complicated challenges. The mental influence of interdisciplinary information includes the increase in mental adaptability, the capability to mix material from several regions, and a complete technique to deal with critical thinking.

Interdisciplinary information transmission likewise cultivates mental coordinated effort, permitting individuals to link disciplinary barriers and engage in cross-disciplinary interchange. The mental modifications involved with interdisciplinary approaches include receptiveness to various points of view, the growth of integrative thinking, and the acceptance of the interconnectivity of knowledge across fields.

Winding about the Strings of Mental Continuity**

The transmission of knowledge and its social influence on insight weave the threads of mental coherence across centuries. From the oral traditions of our progenitors to the technological boondocks of the present, the embroidered artwork of shared astuteness replicates the riches of human thought and the various fashions by which knowledge is handed down and digested.

As we investigate the mind-boggling transaction between information transmission and societal influence, comprehending the unique notion of mental growth is crucial. The transfer of knowledge is not a unidirectional cycle nevertheless a unique exchange that forms both individual personalities and the collective mental landscape of social systems.

In understanding the social influence on cognizance, we welcome the diversity of human thought, the flexibility of social inheritance, and the tremendous power of shared astuteness. The continuing research of information transmission creates roadways for comprehending, coordinated effort, and the continued with growth of the mind-boggling embroidered artwork of human awareness.

8.2 Cognitive Adaptations to Changing Cultural Environments: Navigating the Evolutionary Landscape of the Mind**

The human brain, shaped by a baffling exchange of characteristics and social effects, demonstrates an unusual limit to modification to emerging situations. As societies expand, propelled by inventive headways, social features, and worldwide interconnection, mental changes become important for individuals to prosper within these shifting social scenes. This inquiry looks into the intricate link between mental changes and changing social settings, exploring how the mind explores the developmental problems brought by the strong tapestry of human social orders.

1. Social Development and Mental Flexibility

Social growth, set apart by the transfer of knowledge, beliefs, and ways of acting across ages, demands mental flexibility for individuals to adjust to new norms and ideal models. The capability to explore varied social settings comprises mental cycles related to point of view taking, receptiveness, and the ability to assimilate shifting social cues.

Mental adaptability lets individuals adjust their method of acting, communication styles, and critical thinking approaches in light of the growing assumptions for diverse social contexts. As globalization works with expanded social commerce, mental changes that promote adaptation become vital for pleasant cooperation and the productive path of a socially various planet.

2. Language Elements: Transformation to Multilingual Environments

In changing social situations, phonetic diversity typically occurs as a crucial aspect of variation. People introduced to multilingual situations display mental variations linked with language management, code-exchanging, and the ability to understand and express effectively in diverse phonetic contexts.

The mental influence of multilingualism reaches out beyond etymological powers, influencing mental capabilities linked with leader control, working memory, and metacognition. Variations in language components reflect the brain's capacity to simplify communication operations in light of the social variation encountered in sociable, competent, and instructional circumstances.

3. Mechanical Incorporation: Molding Mental Instrument Use

The rapid synchronization of innovation into social circumstances necessitates mental modifications to investigate sophisticated situations. People should grow skills linked with data proficiency, computerized communication, and the ability to draw in with expanding improvements. Mental changes in light of mechanical reconciliation involve contemplating the board, accomplishing numerous job skills, and the capacity to channel and inspect huge measures of computerized data.

Besides, the utilization of innovation as mental gadgets influences critical thinking methods, inventiveness, and cooperative ventures. The psyche adapts to employ mechanical assets, reshaping mental cycles to match up with the needs of a tech-driven social environment.

4. Web-based Entertainment and Social Cognizance: Exploring On the Web Spaces

The ascension of web-based entertainment has modified the scene of social relationships, asking individuals to adapt intellectually to the complexities of online conversation. Exploring virtual entertainment stages contains the translation of computerized cues, the grasp of online acceptable practices, and the administration of one's advanced character.

Mental differences in the realm of web-based entertainment go out to data management, compassion, and the interchange of online connections. As individuals draw in with varied opinions and encounter facts at a quick pace, the psyche adapts to the remarkable mental wants of virtual social settings.

5. Moving Work Ideal Models: Mental Transformations in the Workplace

Changing socioeconomic circumstances constantly modify the setting of work ideal models. The development from typical office settings to remote work, adjustable schedules, and cooperative computerized stages necessitates mental alterations linked with utilizing time effectively, self-inspiration, and virtual team effort.

Mental cycles linked with critical thinking and navigation go through alterations to fit up with the expanding wants of modern workplaces. The capability to flourish in adaptable work circumstances matches the psyche's potential for mental adjustments because of shifting social assumptions within competent circles.

6. Globalization and Social Insight: Adjusting to Diversity

Globalization stimulates interconnection and social variation, asking for mental alterations as social knowledge. People proficient at researching international social settings demonstrate mental flexibility, social sensitivity, and the potential to genuinely cross social voids.

Social knowledge involves the coordination of various social views, the ability to transmit across social boundaries, and the route of social nuances in different circumstances. The brain changes to turn out to be socially acquainted, supporting successful cooperation and cooperative efforts in a universally connected universe.

7. Social Changes in Schooling: Adjusting Learning Strategies

Social alterations in instructional tactics need mental transformations in learning systems. As educational procedures advance, individuals should shift mental cycles related to data management, decisive thinking, and cooperative learning.

Variations in instructive circumstances may include accepting newly enhanced learning apparatuses, establishing autonomous mastering skills, and acclimating to different educational systems. The brain's potential to react to shifting instructional circumstances parallels its natural flexibility and limits about deep rooted learning.

8. Advancing Standards and Worth Frameworks: Molding Moral Cognition
Social situations continually redefine norms and worth frameworks, inducing mental modifications

in moral perception. People examine moral contemplations, moral predicaments, and evolving cultural beliefs by modifying their ethical reasoning processes.

Mental variations linked with moral awareness incorporate the combining of social attributes, the growth of moral judgment, and the debate of moral challenges within various social structures. The brain's flexibility to change moral reasoning to emerging societal norms contributes to moral dynamism in distinct social contexts.

9. Urbanization and Mental Stressors: Adjusting to City Living

The progress of urbanization poses significant mental pressures linked with city life. People in urban situations could adapt mentally to examine tactile over-burden, quick pace of living, and extended social thickness. Mental alterations in urban environments can include attentional cycles, ways for coping with stress, and the enhancement of flexibility to the mental obstacles given by densely populated and active metropolitan situations.

10. Natural Awareness: Mental Transformations for Sustainability

Developing natural awareness stimulates mental changes related to appropriate living practices. People could promote mental cycles linked with eco-cognizant navigation, natural responsibility, and the incorporation of supportability into day-to-day routines.

Mental variations in light of natural cognizance involve a change in esteem frameworks, the improvement of natural compassion, and the fusion of eco-accommodating methods of behaving into the way of life choices. The psyche's capability to change to a culture of ecological maintainability reflects a mental responsibility to tend to global challenges.

The Powerful Transaction of Culture and Cognition**

The adaptable notion of the human mind is visible in its potential to explore and grow within shifting societal settings. From etymological modifications to mechanical coordination, the psyche continually modifies its mental cycles to line up with the needs of increasing social situations.

The strong interaction of culture and discernment illustrates the proportionate link wherever social situations affect mental alterations, and mental adaptability allows individuals to connect conclusively with various civilizations. As social orders keep on growing, the ongoing dance of culture and discernment adds to the rich woven artwork of human experience, showcasing the variety and flexibility embedded in the complex functions of the brain.

Chapter 9

Contemporary Cognitive Challenges

9.1 Cognitive Evolution in the Modern World

Mental Advancement in the Cutting Edge World: Adjusting Psyches in the Data Age**

The beginning of the 21st century has presented a moment of unmatched development and growth, usually modifying how individuals live, work, and interact. At the center of this exceptional adventure lies the tricky scene of mental improvement, where the human brain adapts to the problems and open doors presented by the cutting-edge environment. From the ubiquity of innovation to the intricacy of global interconnection, this examination digs into the complicated components of mental advancement in the cutting-edge globe, unraveling the flexible tapestry created by brains probing the complexities of the data age.

1. Data Over-burden and Mental Processing

The indication of the cutting-edge world is the rain of data flooding each facet of day-to-day living. The mental evolution stimulated by data over-burden is a display of the psyche's amazing flexibility. People end up growing skills in data sifting, fundamental investigation, and effective decision-production to investigate the large ocean of knowledge. Mental cycles are changed to cope with the continual inflow of data, with thought turning into a valued ware in a world abounding with material.

2. Computerized Proficiency: A New Mental Skillset

In the cutting-edge world, digital education remains a cornerstone of mental growth. As mechanical points of engagement become ubiquitous, the brain adapts to new mental ranges of skills. Exploring computerized environments requires capabilities in web-based communication, data recovery, and the knowledge of sound sources. The mental growth towards computerized education goes beyond plain mechanical skill, developing how individuals think, study, and draw in with the sophisticated scene.

3. Performing multiple jobs and Consideration Management

The sped-up pace of the sophisticated world often needs doing diverse jobs, challenging the brain to adapt to juggling several responsibilities at the same time. Mental growth in this context entails improving the ability to effectively monitor contemplation. The capacity to execute many activities gets intertwined with mental cycles related to focus, memory, and the constant trading between assignments. The cutting-edge mind, in its flexible excursion, refines its capacity to discover an environment requiring synchronous devotion to distinct activities.

4. Virtual Entertainment and the Forming of Social Cognition

The ascension of virtual entertainment has reformed the components of social relationships, motivating a special mental growth in the area of social discernment. Exploring virtual social places involves the modification of mental cycles to interpret sophisticated prompts, understand online usual practices, and curate computerized personalities. Sympathy and interpretation of computerized expressive gestures become key characteristics of mental growth in our contemporary world where social linkages expand beyond actual boundaries.

5. Innovative Reconciliation: Devices as Mental Extensions

The continual merging of innovation into day-to-day existence obscures the boundaries between brain and machine, prompting a fascinating mental growth where exterior instruments become expansions of mental cycles. From cell phones to wearable gadgets, the psyche adapts to mechanical augmentations that boost memory, supply moment access to facts, and operate with communication. Mental progress comprises the combining of these mechanical gadgets into daily mental routines, in a broad sense affecting how individuals observe and interact with the environment.

6. Remote Work and Mental Flexibility

The altering ideal models of jobs, notably the unbounded reception of distant labor, give a unique arrangement of issues needing mental adaptability. People adapt to superior ways of teaming together, supervising time, and keeping up with a balance between entertaining and important tasks in virtual situations. Mental progression in this context incorporates adjustments in communication styles, task association, and the ability to remain on track and helpful exterior typical workplace situations. The sophisticated psyche is excellent at flourishing in adaptable task game designs, revealing its power and limit about variety.

7. Globalization and Social Intelligence

Globalization, a characteristic component of the cutting-edge era, requires mental modifications as social knowledge. The ability to investigate various social situations, both on the web and unconnected, contains altering cerebral cycles to appreciate and esteem alternative points of view. Social knowledge develops into a vital component of mental growth, developing sustainable communication and collaboration in this current world where borders are penetrable, and social variation is applauded.

8. Ecological Mindfulness and Economical Cognition

Developing natural consciousness leads to mental variations toward suitable living behaviors. People progress cognitively to solidify eco-cognizant navigation, taking into consideration the natural consequence of daily choices. Mental growth in this context involves a shift in values, the enhancement of natural compassion, and the merging of eco-accommodating ways of functioning into the way of life choices. The cutting-edge mind grows alert to the importance of maintainability, reflecting a mental responsibility to tend to global challenges.

9. Wellbeing and Prosperity in the Advanced Age

The advanced globe acquaints fresh challenges with wellness and prosperity, with inactive ways of life, screen time, and computerized interruptions becoming widespread concerns. Mental advancement comprises adapting to wellbeing-associated issues via care rehearses, computerized detox procedures, and a mix of innovation for wellbeing checking. The brain evolves to discover some sort of equilibrium between computerized dedication and keeping up with mental and close-to-home prosperity, exhibiting a complex perception of the relationship between innovation and psychological well-being.

10. Moral Contemplations in the Advanced Landscape

The inescapable influence of innovation in the sophisticated world produces moral contemplations that affect mental growth. People examine complicated moral dilemmas linked with protection, information security, and the reliable utilization of innovation. Mental advancement contains the improvement of moral systems and dynamic cycles that square up with the expanding moral scene of the digital era. The cutting-edge intellect wrestles with the confluence of innovation and fundamental quality, exhibiting its aptitude for moral reasoning and trustworthy autonomous orientation.

A Powerful Mental Scene in Flux**

Mental growth in the cutting-edge world is a continual tale, a unique exploration of the brain's suppleness to the continuously changing scenes of the digital age. From the difficulties of data handling to the complexities of moral contemplations in the computerized scene, the cutting-edge mind weaves around an embroidery of mental growth that mimics the adaptability, flexibility, and remarkable possibilities intrinsic to human discernment.

As individuals study the nuances of the cutting-edge world, mental cycles continually go through refining, aligning with the needs of a swiftly expanding scene. The tale of mental growth in the cutting-edge moment is one of variety, study, and the constant goal for harmony on the planet.

9.2 Cognitive Responses to Technological and Social Changes: Navigating the Shifting Landscape**

The cooperative link among innovation and society has presented a moment of spectacular change, shaping the mental scene of individuals in important ways. As mechanical headways and social alterations unfold, the human psyche goes through significant mental responses to examine the unanticipated interplay between progress and cultural movements. This inquiry looks into the various components of mental responses to mechanical and social changes, investigating how the psyche adapts, progresses, and collaborates with the fast-changing reality.

1. Data Over-burden and Mental Filtering

The computerized era is typified by an unceasing expansion of data, offering the human brain the task of coping with an extraordinary amount of information. Mental responses to data over-burden include the advent of separate instruments. People adapt by leveling up talents in understanding significance, concentrating on facts, and establishing a capacity to zero in on vital nuances in the middle of the flood of knowledge. The mental path of separating evolves into a vital competence in exploring the computerized environment, altering how individuals observe, interpret, and apply info.

2. Advanced Education and Mental Flexibility

The mix of innovation into day-to-day existence necessitates a fresh mental range of talents typified by computerized competence. As individuals draw in with varied advanced stages, mental responses include adapting to gradually expanding connection points, equipment, and specialized methods. Computerized schooling improves mental flexibility, permitting individuals to explore new sophisticated situations smoothly. The brain evolves to embrace the swift pace of inventive change, demonstrating a varied mental response to the needs of the advanced period.

3. Virtual Entertainment and Social Mental Adaptations

The rise of online entertainment stages has re-imagined the scene of social connections, stimulating mental responses in the domain of social awareness. People acclimate to the intricacies of online communication, recognizing significant gestures offered in a virtual realm. Social mental modifications involve the grasp of online typical practices, the understanding of computerized sentiments, and the administration of one's advanced personality. The psyche, in light of the commonness of online amusement, refines its social mental cycles to study the nuances of computerized relationships.

4. Performing numerous tasks and Attentional Adjustments

Mechanical progressions have brought an era when executing many activities is much of the time a demand. Mental replies to this requirement include altering attentional cycles to truly manage concurrent tasks. The brain responds by developing the ability to switch between numerous workouts swiftly, assigning consideration decisively, and keeping up with mental execution in executing multiple task scenarios. The mental response to executing several activities parallels the compelling notion of attentional cycles despite rising mechanical and cultural requirements.

5. Remote Work and Mental Resilience

The transition towards remote work, accelerated fast by mechanical progressions, has prompted mental emotions related to work ideal models.

People adjust by producing mental flexibility to the problems of virtual joint effort, time used in adaptable surroundings, and keeping up with central exterior typical workplace circumstances. The mental response to distant work incorporates adjustments in correspondence patterns, the reception of computerized collaboration gadgets, and the creation of mental methodologies to promote efficiency in conveyed work locations.

6. Globalization and Multifaceted Mental Adaptations

Worldwide connection necessitates mental responses that encompass diverse understanding. People adapt by developing social insight and exploring different social contexts both on the web and unconnected. Mental responses to globalization include the coordination of different points of view, the ability to transmit effectively across social bounds, and an understanding of the intricacies of numerous social norms. The psyche grows to turn up to be socially acquainted, demonstrating adaptability despite an inexorably interrelated universe.

7. Moral Contemplations and Moral Reasoning

The mechanical and social modifications provide moral contemplations that form mental responses in moral thought. People examine challenging moral dilemmas associated with protection, information security, and the conscientious utilization of innovation. Mental responses include the enhancement of moral systems, moral dynamic cycles, and an enlarged understanding of the moral repercussions of inventive progressions. The mind responds to the evolving moral scene, demonstrating a heightened sense of duty and moral reasoning even with mechanical and social motions.

8. Natural Mindfulness and Eco-Mental Shifts

Developing natural awareness encourages mental responses related to supportable life behaviors.

People progress intellectually to solidify eco-cognizant orientation, taking into consideration the natural consequence of daily choices. Mental responses include a shift in values, the enhancement of natural compassion, and the merging of eco-accommodating ways of functioning into way of life choices. The brain changes to concentrate on manageability, matching a mental responsibility to responding to global ecological challenges.

9. Wellbeing Tech and Mental Wellness

Headways in wellness innovation short mental responses related to individual prosperity. People adapt by combining well-being monitoring improvements, drawing in with computerized wellness stages, and using mental procedures to keep up with emotional well-being. The mental response to wellness tech incorporates the coordination of innovation as a gadget for taking care of oneself, reflecting a varied perspective that welcomes advances targeted toward upgrading generally speaking prosperity.

10. Mechanical Reliance and Mental Autonomy

As innovation comes out to be increasingly intertwined with day-to-day living, mental replies involve examining the harmony between mechanical reliance and mental freedom. People adapt by building an aware knowledge of their mechanical usage, executing computerized detox approaches, and cultivating snapshots of mental independence. The mental response to mechanical dependence parallels an increasing appreciation of the role of innovation in day-to-day existence and the importance of keeping up with mental organization in an unquestionably tech-driven society.

Decision: A Mental Embroidery Unfolding

Mental responses to mechanical and social changes portray a colorful tapestry of flexibility, plasticity, and progressive evolution. The human mind, in its intricate hit the dance floor with growth and cultural movements, has a startling capacity to evolve, learn, and prosper despite unique changes. From data sifting to moral reasoning, the mental responses represent the intricate exchange between individual personalities and the continually shifting scene of the creative and social circles.

As individuals investigate this complicated and evolving landscape, mental responses become vital threads in the texture of human experience. The narrative of mental variety unfurls as a story of growth, learning, and the constant molding of the psyche in light of the complicated problems and possible open doors brought by the dynamic interchange of innovation and society.

Chapter 10

Future Perspectives

10.1 Emerging Trends in Cognitive Evolution Research

Arising Patterns in Mental Development Exploration: Exploring New Wildernesses of Understanding

Mental advancement study stays at the very front of disentangling the complexity of the human brain's improvement over time. As innovation surges and multidisciplinary approaches acquire evident quality, fresh wildernesses in mental development study occur, offering deeper insights into the progression of human cognizance. This examination looks into the state-of-the-art patterns influencing mental development research, offering insight into the imaginative processes, multidisciplinary coordinated efforts, and unique views that push the field ahead.

1. Interdisciplinary Coordinated Efforts: Spanning Holes in Understanding

One noteworthy feature of mental advancement study includes enhanced collaboration across distinct disciplines. Specialists from domains including humanities, neurology, brain research, hereditary traits, and software engineering are merging to combine pieces of information and build a more far-reaching appreciation of mental growth. Interdisciplinary combined efforts contemplate full research of the different elements affecting mental turn of events, breaking down traditional storehouses and growing a more subtle technique to cope with focusing on the growth of the psyche.

2. Propels in Neuroimaging Advances: Testing the Mind's Depths

Mechanical headways in neuroimaging have changed the inquiry of mental advancement. Utilitarian appealing reverberation imaging (fMRI), magnetoencephalography (MEG), and high-level computational methodologies enable scientists to explore more into the brain substrates of mental cycles. This pattern considers the more precise design of cerebrum parts linked with diverse mental capacities, supplying unusual pieces of information into the neurological variations that have shaped human understanding across transforming time scales.

3. Paleogenomics: Unwinding the Hereditary Strings of Mental Evolution

The science of paleogenomics has witnessed remarkable development, enabling experts to separate and examine outdated DNA. This pattern has huge repercussions for figuring out the genetic underpinning of mental development. By focusing on ancient genomes, scientists may trace the genetic changes that correlate with important breakthroughs in human mental turn of events. Paleogenomics provides a transient aspect to hereditary examination, supplying a one-of-a-kind perspective on the transaction among characteristics and mental changes over different eras.

4. Social Development and Mental Elements: A Two-Way Street

Social growth is gradually seen as a distinctive power shaping mental qualities. The collaboration of social and mental growth is a blossoming trend in the study, highlighting the bidirectional influence of culture and the psyche. This pattern explores how social practices, information transmission, and cultural designs affect the mental turn of events, while also recognizing how mental qualities affect the development of culture. The cooperative connection between culture and understanding exposes fresh levels of complexity in the account of human mental development.

5. Computational Models and Recreations: Virtual Windows into the Past

Computational models and replicas have become outstanding tools in mental progression study. Analysts might generate virtual settings to reproduce developmental scenarios, considering the research of hypotheses and the testing of hypothetical systems. This pattern supplies an essential strategy to cope with usual precise procedures, supplying a dynamic and varied stage for studying the tools that may have powered mental evolution.

6. Longitudinal Investigations: Following Mental Advancement Across Lifetimes

Longitudinal exams, following persons' overstretched durations, have gained notable quality in mental advancement research. This pattern helps scientists to identify mental progress from adolescence to maturity, offering a detailed knowledge of how mental traits evolve during life expectancy. Longitudinal exams supply important information to expose the interchange between hereditary factors, ecological effects, and personal encounters in molding mental directions.

7. Similar Perception: Experiences from Non-Human Species

The examination of mental development reaches beyond persons to incorporate a comparable technique. Analysts increasingly explore the mental capabilities of non-human animals, delivering bits of understanding into the typical and distinctive elements of mental improvement throughout different parts of the transformational tree. Near perception study enlightens the developing underlying foundations of mental qualities, offering a more comprehensive setting for comprehending the diverse advantages and constraints forming mental advancement.

8. Transformative Brain research and Human Way of behaving: Incorporating Perspectives

Transformative brain science goes on taking a significant position in mental development study by looking at how mental qualities contribute to diverse ways of functioning. This pattern blends mental views with transformational structures, studying the advanced components that influence human direction, social relationships, and social behaviors. Developmental brain science supplies a conduct focal point to mental development study, boosting understanding we would interpret the utilitarian significance of mental variations.

9. Resident Science Drives: Drawing in General Society in Discovery

A notable trend incorporates the combining of resident scientific drives with mental development study. Online stages and cooperative ventures link with individuals in general in contributing to knowledge assortment and examination. This democratization of examination considers more expanded collaboration, saddling the aggregate force of varied points of view to settle complicated inquiries in mental growth. Resident scientific urges speed up information assortment as well as promote a sensation of common ownership in the logical inquiry of the psyche's growing excursion.

10. Moral Contemplations: Exploring the Convergence of Science and Values

As brain development research improves, moral contemplations come to the front. Specialists are gradually mindful of the repercussions of their job, including concerns associated with security, acquiescence, and the predicted cultural influence of their findings. This pattern underlines the necessity of skillful examination rehearses and moral frameworks that lead the exploration of the human psyche's transforming history.

Diagramming the Course Ahead**

Arising trends in mental development study demonstrate a discipline in constant progress, reflecting the enormous topic it aims to understand. Interdisciplinary coordinated efforts, mechanical headways, and innovative procedures, all in all, drive the area ahead, revealing new levels of complexity in the account of human mental growth. As specialists study these weird places, the unique transaction involving attributes, culture, and the cerebrum keeps on enrapturing logical requests, promising a future rich with disclosures that will remodel how we can interpret being human.

10.2 Implications for Understanding Human Intelligence: Unraveling the Complex Tapestry of the Mind**

The goal to comprehend human knowledge has been a continual effort, motivated by an inborn curiosity to unwrap the complexity of the mind. As mental science, neurology, and interdisciplinary investigation improve, new experiences occur, modifying the ways we view human knowing. This study digs into the repercussions that fresh advances offer for fathoming human understanding, probing the intricate interchange between inherited characteristics, climate, awareness, and the cultural surroundings that shape our mental skills.

1. Genomics and Insight: Disentangling the Hereditary Code

Late walks in genomics have increased the grasp of the genetic bases of human knowing. The ID of precise attributes linked with mental abilities has expanded repercussions. It not merely gives insight into the heritability of information nevertheless in addition emphasizes the dynamic interaction between hereditary factors and ecological repercussions. This information provides roadways for examining intercessions that could enhance mental turn of affairs and address moral contemplations covering genetic determinants of knowing.

2. Brain Adaptability: Rethinking Insight as a Powerful Process

Progressions in neuroscience have questioned traditional conceptions of knowing as a suitable characteristic. The notion of brain adaptability, the cerebrum's capability to remodel itself due to engagement, argues that knowledge is a dynamic, moldable interaction. This acknowledgment has substantial consequences for schooling and long-lasting picking up, underlining the relevance of enhanced circumstances and varied encounters in encouraging mental growth all through life expectancy.

3. Ecological Impacts: Sustaining Knowledge in Context

Understanding human understanding entails acknowledging the significant influence of ecological factors. Financial standing, entrance to instruction, and social encounters affect mental turn of events. Ongoing inquiry stresses the importance of establishing environments that nurture academic interest, supplying evenhanded instructional open doors, and understanding the function of cultural surroundings in forming various appearances of knowing throughout altered social settings.

4. Various Insights Hypothesis: Past IQ

Howard Gardner's idea of multiple insights questions the customary emphasis on a specific, unitary knowledge evaluated by the level of IQ testing. This shift in viewpoint acknowledges the existence of multiple mental faculties, including phonetic, spatial, melodic, relational, and intrapersonal insights. The consequences extend out to instructional works, stressing a more expanded scope of skills and abilities that amount to a far-reaching grasp of human insight.

5. The ability to appreciate others on a fundamental level: Incorporating Feelings into the Intellect

The acknowledgment of the capacity to understand individuals on a profound level as a particular feature of human knowledge has groundbreaking ramifications for relational elements and individual achievement. This perspective underlines the capacity to comprehend and deal with feelings, explore social connections actually, and pursue informed choices in light of close-to-home mindfulness. The mix of the ability to understand anyone on a deeper level into conversations on knowledge grows the components of being mentally skilled in the intricacies of human collaborations.

6. Social Predisposition in Knowledge Testing: Tending to Diversity

The ongoing talk features the social predisposition intrinsic to customary knowledge tests. The ramifications for understanding human knowledge include perceiving and moderating inclinations that may unreasonably inconvenience people from specific social foundations. Endeavors to foster socially fair evaluations and consider a more extensive cluster of mental abilities add to a more comprehensive and exact comprehension of insight across different populations.

7. Man-made brainpower and Human Cognizance: Cooperative energies and Challenges
The approach of man-made consciousness (artificial intelligence) presents two open doors and

difficulties for grasping human insight. Simulated intelligence frameworks, roused by human mental cycles, give an interesting focal point through which to concentrate on knowledge. On the other hand, the moral ramifications of simulated intelligence, including worries about work removal and protection, require a more profound comprehension of the human parts of insight. The convergence among counterfeit and human insight prompts reflection on the quintessence of awareness, imagination, and moral navigation.

8. Knowledge as a Powerful Organization: Network in the Brain
Headways in cerebrum imaging advancements have worked with a shift towards grasping knowledge as

a powerful organization of interconnected locales. Utilitarian network studies uncover complex examples of correspondence between various cerebrum regions during mental undertakings. This pattern holds suggestions for distinguishing brain marks of insight, making ready for additional designated intercessions, and offering a more profound comprehension of how different mental cycles cooperatively add to generally learned capacities.

9. Life Expectancy Improvement: Insight Across Ages

A life expectancy viewpoint on insight research has acquired an unmistakable quality, taking into account mental changes from the earliest stages through advanced age. Longitudinal examinations uncover the direction of mental turn of events, distinguishing basic times of progress and expected intercessions to help mental well-being across life expectancy. The ramifications stretch out to instructive systems, mental mediations, and cultural intending to oblige the developing necessities of people at various phases of life.

10. Moral Contemplations in Knowledge Exploration: Effects and Responsibilities
As insight research advances, moral contemplations become central. The ramifications reach out to issues of assent, protection, and expected abuse of insight-related information. Analysts bear the

obligation of guaranteeing that their discoveries contribute emphatically to society, keeping away from deterministic accounts, and perceiving the variety of human potential. The moral aspect highlights the requirement for straightforwardness, inclusivity, and a pledge to the prosperity of people and networks impacted by insight research.

Exploring the Consistently Unfurling Odyssey of Intelligence**

Understanding human insight is a consistently developing odyssey, set apart by the assembly of hereditary qualities, neuroscience, brain science, and cultural elements. Late patterns highlight the dynamic, complex nature of insight, testing assumptions and opening new vistas for investigation. The ramifications reach out to past scholarly communities, affecting instruction, strategy-making, and cultural perspectives toward knowledge. As we explore this perplexing embroidery of the mind, the journey for a more significant comprehension of human knowledge keeps on enthralling the creative mind, promising a future where the extravagance of mental variety is praised and utilized to improve mankind.

Chapter 11

Conclusioons

Significance of Continued Research in Cognitive Evolution

The Meaning of Proceeded with Exploration in Mental Development: Disclosing the Secrets of the Mind

Mental advancement study stays as a dynamic and necessary discipline, continually pushing the bounds of how we may understand the human psyche's improvement over time. The significance of continual examination in mental growth goes a long way past scholarly curiosity, altering various components of society, training, and our aggregate grasp of being human. This investigation dives into the critical importance of supported study into mental growth, assessing its recommendations for logical progression, instruction, and a more comprehensive cultural account.

1. Opening the Insider Truths of Human Origins

Proceeded with study in mental development fills in as a critical feature for exposing the secrets of human beginning points. By emphasizing the evolutionary orientations of mental faculties, analysts may track the fundamental foundations of uniquely human traits, for example, sophisticated critical thinking, language, and social discernment. Understanding these beginnings offers insights into the unmistakable mental qualities that have shaped human growth, dividing our species into the creatures of the globe collectively.

2. Enlightening the Exchange of Nature and Nurture

Mental development study gives insight into the confusing interchange between hereditary factors and environmental effects in establishing mental talents. Researching how attributes and the atmosphere help mental growth increases how we can perceive the strong notion of insight. This knowledge has down-to-earth uses in training, as it underlines the necessity of building better environments that support mental growth and tackle inequalities in admission to instructional open doors.

3. Progressing Instructive Practices

Research in mental development reveals and develops instructional techniques. By realizing the variety of mental capacities and learning styles, instructors may adjust educational tactics to gratify the altered wants of understudies. Understanding the transforming foundations of perception likewise aids in the improvement of instructional intercessions that advance ideal learning settings, fostering the scholastic development of individuals throughout different progressive phases.

4. Encouraging Mechanical Innovations

The pieces of information gathered from the mental development study assume a position in encouraging mechanical improvements. As we widen how we perceive human understanding, we might nurture inventions that match up with the regular thought cycles of individuals. This commemorates headways for human-PC connection, man-made reasoning, and the design of simple-to-utilize improvements that impact our mental assets. The cooperative energy between mental exploration and mechanical development might potentially transform the method in which we draw in and profit from inventive headways.

5. Tending to Cultural Challenges

Mental development research advises caring for cultural issues. By knowing the mental foundations of autonomous direction, cooperation, and communication, scientists may give major pieces of information to areas like public approach, social aspects, and compromise. This knowledge offers society a more sophisticated grasp of the human method of behaving, taking into account evidence-based strategies to deal with complicated challenges and promote favorable societal consequences.

6. Improving Psychological Well-being Interventions

Research in mental advancement contributes to the development of emotional well-being mediations. By uncovering the developmental foundations of mental cycles linked with pressure, flexibility, and deep guidance, experts might highlight helpful approaches that line up with our advanced mental systems. This has pragmatic repercussions for the improvement of mediations to handle emotional well-being concerns, focusing on general prosperity and adaptability despite life's obstacles.

7. Exploring Mechanical and Social Shifts

As society goes through swift mechanical and social motions, continued study in mental development becomes important. The experiences acquired from this investigation aid individuals and networks in understanding the nuances of a fast-altering environment. Whether it's adapting to new communication advances or recognizing the mental consequences of social alterations, continual investigation supplies a guide to effectively investigating the problems and useful open doors provided by changing cultural scenes.

8. Protecting Mental Diversity

Research in mental development underlines the relevance of mental variability within the human species. By noticing and commending the scope of mental talents that have progressed over the long haul, we promote a thorough appreciation of insight. This has societal consequences for increasing variation and consideration, checking generalizations, and developing situations that respect the particular commitments of persons with fluctuating mental characteristics and points of view.

9. Moral Contemplations in Science and Technology

Proceeded with study in mental development underlines the relevance of moral contemplations in logical request and mechanical progressions. As we delve more into the secrets of the brain, moral standards become vital to guarantee reliable exploration rehearses, defend the liberties of research participants, and relieve prospective cultural risks linked with the utilization of mental pieces of information in different areas.

10. Motivating Interest and Long lasting Learning

The continual exploration of mental growth drives curiosity and cultivates a culture of long-lasting learning. As scientists unveil new elements of our mental history, the narrative of human understanding evolves into an enrapturing and unfolding drama. This narrative can pull in individuals across ages, promoting a sensation of amazement, attention, and a vow to continually seek more about the subtleties of the human mind.

A Constant Excursion of Discovery**

All in all, the notion of continuing study in mental growth reaches a great ways over the confines of logical request. It concerns education, innovation, cultural prosperity, and the real texture of being human. The mysteries of the mind keep on seducing scientists on a continual expedition of disclosure, offering a future where how we can understand mental growth enhances diverse characteristics of human existence. As we explore this academic voyage, the significance resides in the replies we reveal as well as in the queries that propel us onward, ensuring that the hunt for knowledge remains a persevering and breakthrough force.

www.ingramcontent.com/pod-product-compliance
Lightning Source LLC
Chambersburg PA
CBHW070821250726
48662CB00003B/1042